HOW TO READ
PAUL

HOW TO READ
PAUL

A Brief Introduction to His Theology, Writings, and World

YUNG SUK KIM

FORTRESS PRESS
MINNEAPOLIS

HOW TO READ PAUL
A Brief Introduction to His Theology, Writings, and World

Cover image: © 2020; CC BY-SA 3.0; Paul the Apostle (https://tinyurl.com/y2jxo4nw) by Alexey Yushenkov

Cover design: Alisha Lofgren

Print ISBN: 978-1-5064-7144-0
eBook ISBN: 978-1-5064-7145-7

I dedicate this book to three distinguished professors
at Samuel DeWitt Proctor School of Theology,
Virginia Union University, in Richmond, Virginia:

Dr. John W. Kinney, Distinguished Professor of Theology

Dr. Boykin Sanders, Distinguished Professor
of New Testament Studies and Greek

Dr. James Henry Harris, Distinguished Professor
of Homiletics and Pastoral Theology and
Research Scholar in Religion and Humanities

CONTENTS

ACKNOWLEDGMENTS

During the past fifteen years, I have taught passionately about Paul and examined conscientiously critical topics in Paul's letters. This book represents the fruit of my hard work over a long period of my teaching and research. I give my special thanks to my school (Samuel DeWitt Proctor School of Theology at Virginia Union University), Dean Greg Howard, the faculty, the staff, and especially, my students. I cannot enumerate all levels of support and love I have received from them. Dr. Boykin Sanders is a senior New Testament scholar and an inspiration for my teaching and scholarship. Dr. James Harris, a senior professor of homiletics, always supports my work and scholarship. We often engage in various topics in the Bible and talk about preaching issues. Dr. Robert Wafawa-naka, associate professor of Hebrew Bible, is a rare faculty member who is committed to nurturing students. He read my full manuscript and affirmed it with encouraging words. I have been blessed with my students who took my classes on the New Testament. Their questions and desire to learn more about Paul motivated me to write this book.

At the 2019 Annual Meeting of Society of Biblical Litera-ture (SBL) in San Diego, I came to conceive of this book and shared my book idea with Scott Tunseth, general editor at Fortress. He encouraged me to pursue this book with a focus on preaching Paul. I did it. But it did not go well because my book lacked preaching elements. But he encouraged me to come back with a new proposal anytime. Taking some time, I decided to write a textbook for college and graduate students. The new proposal was redirected to Ryan Hemmer, acquisitions editor for theology and biblical studies at Fortress. Soon, I heard that the publications committee unanimously approved my proposal for publication. I was so excited and felt welcomed once again, since my first book, *Christ's Body in Corinth: The Politics of a Metaphor*, was published by Fortress in 2008. I give my special thanks to Scott Tunseth and Ryan Hemmer at Fortress Press.

At the SBL meeting in San Diego last year, I also met a few of my colleagues and shared my book idea with them. I talked with Troy Troftgruben, associate professor of New Testament at Wartburg Theological Seminary. Later, he read my full manuscript and gave me critical comments and tips to revise. Through his help, I rethought my book's audience and purpose. I also talked with Daniel Smith, associate professor of New Testament at Saint Louis University. He introduced his new book *Into the World of the New Testament* to me, and it was very helpful. He read my full manuscript and gave me helpful feedback on the Greco-Roman and Jewish texts. I am very much thankful for his genuine support for me. I also had a great time with Ekaputra Tupamahu, assistant professor of New Testament at Portland Seminary and George Fox University. He listened to my project carefully and encouraged me to continue to follow my dream. I also had pleasant conversations with Kang-Yup Na, professor of New Testament at Westminster College. I thank him for his support and encouragement. I also had a very open discussion with Jung Choi, assistant professor of religious studies at North Carolina Wesleyan College. I thank her for her wisdom and support of my project. I would also like to thank Carla Works, associate professor of New Testament at Wesley Theological Seminary, who read my full manuscript and gave me positive feedback.

Lastly, what I am now is because of my family's dedication and love. I thank my wife, YongJeong, for her dedication to our family members. I am so proud of my daughters for their trust in me: HyeRim, HyeKyung, and HyeIn.

INTRODUCTION

Oftentimes I hear from my academic circles or from the communities to which I belong, "Jesus is yes, but Paul is no!" Some people say that while Jesus taught the kingdom of God in the world, Paul did not teach what Jesus taught. They also say Paul taught only about Jesus and his death. So, for them, Paul is not considered a true follower of Jesus. However, this view does not seem fair. Paul also emphasized God's good news (Rom 1:1), God's righteousness (Rom 1:17; 3:21–26), and God's power (Rom 1:16; 1 Cor 1:25), which must be realized in the world. As Jesus took care of the poor and oppressed, Paul also had concern for them.[1] During his ministry, Paul was concerned about economic security for poor people and collected money to help them (1 Cor 16:1–4; 2 Cor 8:1–9:15; Rom 15:14–32). He also emphasized a fair balance between the abundant and the destitute throughout his communities (2 Cor 8:13–15), quoting from Exod 16:18: "The one who had much did not have too much, and the one who had little did not have too little" (2 Cor 8:15). During his missionary journeys, he worked hard with his hands in solidarity with those who were marginalized.

Others say Paul is a social conservative. Obviously, he is not a radical, political revolutionary, and neither is Jesus for

---

1. See Carla Works, *The Least of These: Paul and the Marginalized* (Grand Rapids: Eerdmans, 2020), 1–11. Works argues that Paul should be seen as an apostle who had a passion for helping the marginalized: the poor at Jerusalem, slaves, the marginalized women, and other poor gentiles.

that matter. Though not an abolitionist, Paul does not promote slavery.[2] As an apocalyptic thinker, he believes God will
eventually intervene in the world and rectify what is wrong
there. Paul's view of gender, marriage, or society is influenced
by this apocalyptic view. Though his theology is apocalyptic, he still emphasizes the "already but not yet" theology that
teaches that people can experience God's power here in the
world. He does not delay the fruit of the Spirit to the future
(Gal 5:22–23). Those who follow Jesus may experience a new
life of righteousness, peace, and justice in the here and now.

Still others say that Paul is a betrayer of Judaism. But in
Romans, he makes it clear that faith cannot overthrow the
law, which is holy and perfect (Rom 3:31; 7:12). Furthermore,
he says God did not abandon his people yet because of their
faithlessness now (Rom 3:3; 11:28–30). He hopes for the salvation of Israel through Jesus and faith, as he says, "And so all
Israel will be saved; as it is written, 'Out of Zion will come the
Deliverer; he will banish ungodliness from Jacob'" (Rom 11:26).
Paul did not judge God's people on the basis of their present
reality.

There are so many things that we need to deconstruct and
reconstruct about Paul, partly because he was misunderstood
and partly because his gospel was not thoroughly or holistically explicated. We need to reexamine Paul's letters and
his theology and learn something fresh from him. He is not
a naive thinker but a critical theologian who tries to communicate the good news of God to the gentiles, especially to the
marginalized who do not have a voice or share in the world.
For this purpose, he articulates God, the Messiah Jesus, the
Holy Spirit, and many related themes such as righteousness,
faith, freedom, and community. He has a down-to-earth

---

2. According to Brad Braxton, Paul, in 1 Cor 7:17–24, does not promote slavery; rather,
he emphasizes God's call of the Corinthians in Christ and his liberative power with which
they must remain (1 Cor 7:24). See Brad Braxton, No Longer Slaves: Galatians and African-
American Experience (Collegeville, MN: Liturgical, 2002), 28–53. See also Brad Braxton, The
Tyranny of Resolution: 1 Cor 7:17–24 (Atlanta: Society of Biblical Literature, 1999), 220–34.
See also Yung Suk Kim, Christ's Body in Corinth: The Politics of a Metaphor (Minneapolis:
Fortress, 2008), 58.

perspective on salvation, as he talks about God's radical love for the most marginalized: "God chose what is foolish in the world to shame the wise; God chose what is weak in the world to shame the strong" (1 Cor 1:27).

This book comes out of my passion for teaching. I love Paul and his letters not because he is a "perfect" apostle or theologian but because he has a passion for the good news of God for the gentiles (Rom 1:1–17). The good news comes from God, and it is about God. The good news is that God is love, peace, and justice and that people may live a new life as children of God. They may find new meaning in life and keep hope in God. They may not give in to hopelessness. For Paul, the good news is not an idea or the otherworldly phantom that is realized only in a discrete future. The good news must be practical and experienced in the present. Jesus as Son of God proclaimed and exemplified the good news of God until he died. In other words, God's mercy, love, and justice were fully effective for people through Jesus's faithfulness. He was faithful to the will of God, who loved the world. Because of Christ's grace and love, God declared a new time of salvation or reconciliation (Rom 3:21–26). The good news is that now God justifies the one who has the faithfulness of Jesus (Rom 3:26). This means the right relationship with God is based on Christlike faith. One may live a new life in Christ and be given a new message to proclaim, which is none other than the good news of God proclaimed by Christ. The followers of Jesus are a letter of Christ (2 Cor 3:3), and they have to spread the good news of Christ, dying with him, living to God, being led by the Spirit. If they are not led by the Spirit, they are not children of God (Rom 8:14). Their task is to demonstrate God's love and justice in the world.

However, many misunderstand Paul or poorly interpret him. Indeed, he is difficult to understand, not to mention to preach, because he is usually understood from the perspective of all thirteen letters traditionally attributed to him.[3] In fact, the thirteen letters attributed to Paul do not

---

3. Paul's seven undisputed letters are often called "authentic letters," and they are as follows: Romans, 1 Corinthians, 2 Corinthians, Galatians, Philippians, 1 Thessalonians, and

say the same things. For example, marriage is discouraged in 1 Corinthians, but it is encouraged in the Pastoral letters. Whereas in Paul's undisputed letters, women are free to participate in worship and church (1 Cor 11:5),[4] they should not teach over men in the Pastoral letters (1 Tim 2:11–15). Paul, in his authentic letters, clearly states that the Christian *ekklesia*

Philemon. The debatable or disputable letters of Paul come in two categories: Deutero-Pauline Letters (2 Thessalonians, Colossians, and Ephesians) and Pastoral letters (1 Timothy, 2 Timothy, and Titus). While the authorship of Paul in the former category is still debatable, that in the latter category is disputed. We will see the differences between Paul's authentic letters and later epistles in the next two chapters.

4. Among Paul's undisputed letters, 1 Cor 14:33b–36 is an exception, and it is considered an interpolation, which means an inserted text from a later editor. This text is similar to 1 Tim 2:11–14, which is part of the Pastoral letters that reflect post-Pauline theology and issues. Namely, the churches became very conservative after Paul and adopted the social convention of social hierarchy, including gender hierarchy. Otherwise, within Paul's undisputed letters, except for 1 Cor 14:33b–36, there are no women-degrading texts. Rather, the opposite is the case. Paul had fellow women leaders such as Phoebe, Prisca, and Junia. Junia was called among the foremost apostles (Rom 16:7). Some may say 1 Cor 11:2–16 is evidence that Paul has a negative view of women. But this claim is arguable, since there are diverse opinions. As I wrote elsewhere, regarding disputes over women's head covering (1 Cor 11:1–16), there are diverse views: (1) Paul's concern about gender confusion due to women's hairstyle, (2) Paul's concern about radical gender equality, (3) Paul's concern about the disturbing acts by some women with pagan worshiping styles, (4) this text is an interpolation, (5) Paul quotes the hegemonic voice of the opponents in 11:4–7 to counter it, and (6) Paul's affirmation of the marginalized women who also deserve head covering, since it is honorable. For an overall view of the diverse scholarly views, see Antoinette Wire, *The Corinthian Women Prophets: A Reconstruction through Paul's Rhetoric* (Minneapolis: Fortress, 1990), 220–23. Regarding view 1 mentioned previously, see C. K. Barrett, *A Commentary on the First Epistle to the Corinthians* (New York: Harper and Row, 1968), 249–51. For view 2, see Jouette Bassler, "1 Corinthians," in *Women's Bible Commentary*, ed. Carol Newsom and Sharon Ringe (Louisville: Westminster John Knox, 1998), 416–17. For view 3, see Jerome O'Connor-Murphy, "1 Corinthians 11:2–16 Once Again," *Catholic Biblical Quarterly* (hereafter CBQ) 50 (1988): 265–74. For view 4, see Garry W. Trompf, "On Attitudes toward Women in Paul and Paulinist Literature: 1 Corinthians 11:3–16 and Its Context," CBQ 42 (1980): 196–215. See also Wm. O. Walker, "1 Corinthians and Paul's Views regarding Women," *Journal of Biblical Literature* (hereafter JBL) 94 (1974): 94–110. For view 5, see David Odell-Scott, *Paul's Critique of Theocracy: A/Theocracy in Corinthians and Galatians* (New York: T&T Clark, 2003), 168–72. See also, David Odell-Scott, "Let the Women Speak in Church: An Egalitarian Interpretation of 1 Cor 14:33b–36," *Biblical Theology Bulletin* 13 (1983): 90–93. For view 6, see Works, *Least of These*, 55–68.

("gathering" or "church") is an egalitarian community in Christ (Gal 3:28) and that both women and men participate in worship freely (1 Cor 11) and receive the gifts of the Spirit equally (1 Cor 12–14). According to Paul, women were church leaders. Phoebe served as "a deacon [*diakonos*] of the church in Cenchreae" (Rom 16:1). Here, *diakonos* is not the laity but a minister responsible for the local church. Priscilla, along with her husband, Aquila, was a coworker of Paul (Rom 16:3–5; Acts 18:1–3). Junia was an apostle along with her husband, Andronicus (Rom 16:7). But in the Deutero-Pauline and Pastoral letters, the church becomes conservative, and suddenly, women are not allowed to teach or become leaders of the church (1 Tim 2:11–15). The famous "household codes" in these letters are good examples of the church being concerned with order and survival under the harsh world of the Roman Empire.[5] In these codes, slavery is taken for granted and slaves must obey their masters.[6] Given these differences mentioned previously, we can hardly reconcile two different Pauls here. So,

5. Household codes (Eph 5:22–6:9; Col 3:18–4:1; 1 Tim 2:10–15; 5:1–6:2; 2 Tim 2:20–22) reflect the later church's need to deal with its internal and external issues regarding "relationship" rules. As the Parousia did not come right away, the church needed to maintain its status and survive harsh persecutions while accepting the social convention of hierarchical relationships among different social members: relationships between parents and children, between masters and slaves, and between genders. The church also dealt with radical egalitarianism and did not allow for radical equality in the church. Yet the good function of these household codes in the church has to do with mutual bonds within the community in times of crisis. With this role of internal solidarity, the church could deal with external issues such as persecution or other hardships. At the same time, the church could grow because society did not see it as strange or antisocial. Nevertheless, the previously mentioned household codes imply that a sense of egalitarian community, as in Gal 3:28, faded. See Bart Ehrman, *The New Testament: A Historical Introduction to the Early Christian Writings* (New York: Oxford University Press, 2016), 444–45.

6. Regarding slavery in early Christianity, see Mitzi J. Smith, "Slavery in the Early Church," in *True to Our Native Land: An African American Commentary of the New Testament*, ed. Brian Blount et al. (Minneapolis: Fortress, 2007), 11–22. See also Jennifer Glancy, *Slavery in Early Christianity* (Minneapolis: Fortress, 2006). See also Dale Martin, *Slavery as Salvation: The Metaphor of Slavery in Pauline Christianity* (New Haven: Yale University Press, 1990). Regarding poverty in early Christianity, see Justin Meggitt, *Paul, Poverty, and Survival* (Edinburgh: T&T Clark, 1998). Regarding the concept of the body and body politics, see Dale Martin, *The Corinthian Body* (New Haven: Yale University Press, 1995).

in order to understand Paul correctly, we must depend on his seven authentic letters.[7]

What is more complicated is Acts' description of Paul. In Acts, Paul appears as an eloquent public preacher who is talking with philosophers in Athens, at the Areopagus, and meets Jewish people at the synagogue (Acts 17:16–34). But in his letters, we see a very different Paul whose primary contact is not Jews or elite leaders but everyday people of gentile origin (1 Cor 1:26–28; 1 Thess 2:9). Overall, in Acts, Paul is portrayed as an ideal apostle, sent by the Holy Spirit and endorsed by the Jerusalem apostles.[8] This image of Paul differs from his letter to the Galatians, for example. Here, he says his ministry was spied on by certain people who came from James, the head of the Jerusalem church (Gal 2:12). He had a conflict with Peter, who came to Antioch and withdrew from the table fellowship with the gentiles.

The other factor contributing to the difficulty of understanding Paul has to do with the unspeakable amount of interpretation about him.[9] Next is a list of important interpretive questions about him:

- Is he a systematic theologian who paves a new way of salvation based on "faith in Christ"?

- Is he a social conservative or a challenger to the Roman Empire?

---

7. This book does not argue that Paul's seven "authentic" letters are systematic treatises that hold clear positions. Strictly speaking, they are also "occasional" treatises that deal with the concerns of a particular community. Nevertheless, his letters reveal the core of his theological thinking, and this book seeks to explore key theological concepts by carefully examining all his undisputed letters.

8. The major differences between Paul's undisputed letters and Acts are as follows: (1) Paul is for the gentiles, and Acts for Jews first; (2) Paul has a rough relationship with the Jerusalem church, but Acts says Paul's relationship with the Jerusalem church is good; (3) in Romans, all people knew God, but in Acts, the gentiles were ignorant of God; and (4) Paul never mentions his citizenship status in his letters, but Acts says he is a Roman citizen.

9. To see a wide array of approaches to Paul, see Magnus Zetterholm, *Approaches to Paul: A Student's Guide to Recent Scholarship* (Minneapolis: Fortress, 2009).

- What is his view of the law and Israel?

- What is his view of Jesus and his death?

- What are his views of God, the Abrahamic covenant, and the children of God?

- What is his view of faith and the law?

- What does he mean by "the righteousness of God"?

- How can one be justified by God? By one's faith in Christ or through Christ's faith?

- What kind of gospel does he proclaim to the gentiles?

- What are his views of community, gender, class, or ethnicity?

- What is his view of society or the governing authorities?

- What is his relationship with the Jerusalem church?

- What is his primary identity after following Jesus?

- How does his Diaspora experience affect his gospel?

Paul is one of the most controversial figures in the history of Christianity. On the one hand, he has been claimed as a champion of the Christian gospel and the founder of Christianity. So much so that Rom 1:17 and Gal 2:16, among other texts, have been read to support the doctrine of "justification by faith." The basis of justification is by faith in Christ whose vicarious sacrifice made perfect atonement once and for all. Usually, in this reading, faith is set against the law or Judaism. In some Christian circles, Paul was understood as anti-Jewish. Marcion, a second-century CE heretic, thought that Paul rejected the law and Judaism. Some gentile Christians tended to understand Paul in that way and ignored the Jewish law. On the other hand, some Jewish followers of Jesus such as Ebionites rejected Paul because he was an apostate from the law.[10] Overall, Paul's gospel has dominated Christian

10. See Irenaeus, *Against Heresies*, Early Christian Writings, accessed September 28, 2020, 1.26.2, https://tinyurl.com/oaj4c6b.

discourse throughout history. He became an authority in the church, and his signature teaching was summarized with justification by faith and unity in the body of Christ. On the flip side, Paul's emphases on the diversity of cultures and equality among genders and ethnicities were either ignored or underemphasized. Likewise, there was no serious discussion about faith as participation in Jesus or engagement in the world.[11]

Even with the difficulties of understanding him, some things are clear from his letters. Paul vehemently states that he cannot overthrow the law by faith. Rather, he says, "We uphold the law" (Rom 3:31; cf. 7:12, 14; Gal 5:14).[12] He even says in Rom 11:26, "All Israel will be saved." Apparently, he is not anti-Jewish or antinomian, and he does not say that the law is wrong (Gal 3:21). E. P. Sanders points out that Jews also believed in the grace of God and stayed in the covenantal community because of God's covenant with them.[13]

---

11. John Barclay, *Paul and the Gift* (Grand Rapids: Eerdmans, 2017). Still, the majority of Christians and scholars take *pistis christou* as "faith in Christ." But an increasing number of scholars these days take it as Christ's faithfulness. We will get back to this issue in the next chapters. The Common English Bible (CEB) reflects this new scholarship (see Rom 3:22; Gal 2:16). Rom 3:22 CEB reads, "God's righteousness comes through *the faithfulness of Jesus Christ* for all who have faith in him. There's no distinction" (italics mine). Also, Gal 2:16 CEB reads, "However, we know that a person isn't made righteous by the works of the Law but rather through *the faithfulness of Jesus Christ*. We ourselves believed in Christ Jesus so that we could be made righteous by *the faithfulness of Christ* and not by the works of the Law—because no one will be made righteous by the works of the Law" (italics mine).

12. Paul's view of the law here is similar to Jesus in Matt 5:17: "Do not think that I have come to abolish the law or the prophets; I have come not to abolish but to fulfill."

13. E. P. Sanders, *Paul and Palestinian Judaism: A Comparison of Patterns of Religion* (Philadelphia: Fortress, 1977), 419–30. Sanders introduced the term *covenantal nomism*, which characterizes Palestinian Judaism in the first century CE. The term means Jews are covenantal people and keep the law not to earn righteousness but to stay in the covenantal community as a people of God. The old perspective on Judaism and Paul is challenged because Judaism in the first century is not a legalistic religion. It is also the religion of grace. God made a covenant with Abraham and gave the law for blessing his descendants. God loved them, and therefore, they kept the law. They became children of God already. They do not keep the law to be justified or to become his people. In response to God's love or covenant, they keep the law and stay in a covenantal community. Therefore, in this view, Paul did not leave Judaism or the law. In fact, he affirms the law (Rom 3:29–31; 7:12) and the place of Israel (Rom 9–11). His point is not that one must be justified by such a faith alone

The question, then, as Sanders asks, is, "What, in Paul's view, was wrong with Judaism?"[14] He gives his own answer to this question: "This is what Paul finds wrong in Judaism: it is not Christianity." But this answer needs explaining. In my view, Sanders does not touch on Paul's scriptural reasoning about the law and faith. Paul's premier argument in Rom 4 is as follows: faith comes before the law; and eventually what comes first is the grace of God, as in Abraham's story in Gen 12. The problem for Jews, in Paul's understanding, is that they began with the story of circumcision in Gen 17 and absolutized the law without seeing the importance of faith. The interpretation of Jews is not wrong from their perspective. So what we see here are two different interpretations of Abraham's story. Paul does not oppose the law per se, which is the gift of God for the Israelites. They are covenanted people and need to maintain a peaceful, law-abiding community. In Paul's view, however, the foundation of their community should not be the law but rather Christ, who fulfilled God's promise given to Abraham (Gal 3–4). Paul's point is that the law should not be the starting point of their interpretation. What they need is faith and to keep the law through Christ or faith. In other words, the purpose of the law is love, especially the love of neighbor, as Paul says in Gal 5:14 and Rom 13:8–10. If one has faith or trust in God, that person should love their neighbor. In other words, the issue is not about choosing faith or the law.

Paul takes one step further and argues that Jesus, who was crucified on the cross, is the Messiah (Christ), the Son of God, who confirmed the promise of God made to Abraham. Jesus revealed God's love through his faithfulness and fulfilled the law (Rom 10:4). This does not mean the law is outdated or

---

but that both Jews and gentiles can stand in the right relationship with God. That is through faith that Jesus showed. In this view, Jesus fulfilled the law. The problem for Jews is their rejection of Jesus as the Messiah and their narrow interpretation of the law, which is shown in their zeal for God. Calvin Roetzel summarizes a perspective on Paul: "It is not bad Torah that brings to sin and death . . . but rather the crooked human heart." See Calvin Roetzel, *The Letters of Paul* (Louisville: Westminster John Knox, 1998), 116.

14. Roetzel, *Letters of Paul*, 116.

imperfect. His point is that Christ Jesus revealed who God is and fulfilled the law in the way of love of neighbor. In the end, Sanders's observation about Paul may be correct, but we need to see Paul's distinctive scriptural interpretation of the law and faith.

We need to hear what Paul says to us rather than what we want to hear from him. Many people think that the centerpiece of Paul's gospel is "justification by faith." But his gospel is more complex than that and can be understood in diverse ways.[15] For Paul, the gospel may be a message about God or Jesus. It may be the power of God for salvation to all who have faith (Rom 1:16). It may be the work of Jesus or the Holy Spirit's role in the lives of Christians. In all of these, the skeleton of Paul's gospel is "God-centered, Christ-exemplified, and Christian-imitated."[16] Initially, the good news was given to Abraham and his descendants, and it was about blessings for his descendants and their prosperity. Ultimately, this good news was confirmed through Jesus and made available for all who come to Jesus, which means participating in his faithfulness.[17] Paul's gospel starts with God, who is the source of our life, our hope, and our

15. Graham Twelftree examines the polyvalence of Paul's gospel that includes the following: "tradition about Jesus, Jesus Christ himself, the ministry of Jesus, the replication of the ministry of Jesus, God's salvific drama, the salvation experience of people, a message, and something that can (and should) be lived." Graham Twelftree, *The Gospel According to Paul: A Reappraisal* (Eugene, OR: Cascade, 2019), 193.

16. In my recent publication titled *Rereading Romans from the Perspective of Paul's Gospel* (Eugene, OR: Resource, 2019), I articulated the threefold gospel that involves God's good news, Christ's good news, and Christians' proclamation of the gospel. That is, to Paul's gospel, Christ's faithfulness is important along with Christians' participation in him. Yet, in the field, it is hard to see this emphasis on Christ's faithfulness. For example, the authors of the book *Preaching Romans: Four Perspectives* (Grand Rapids: Eerdmans, 2019) rarely consider Christ's faithfulness while dealing with four different perspectives on Paul: the Lutheran reading of Paul, the New Perspective, the apocalyptic reading, and the participationist perspective.

17. In my recent work, Galatians is outlined with the theme of the gospel under which all other topics come: justification, new life, new creation, freedom, faith, sin, or the law. See Yung Suk Kim, *Rereading Galatians from the Perspective of Paul's Gospel* (Eugene, OR: Cascade, 2019). Romans can be also outlined with the same theme of the gospel. See Kim, *Rereading Romans*.

trust.[18] God is the beginning of the good news. Paul's gospel or theology or mission begins with God, who revealed his Son to him (Gal 1:15–16). Jesus Christ is the Son of God, who proclaimed God's good news. He disclosed God's righteousness and extended his covenantal love to all. Jesus is the good news. God acknowledges his grace and sacrifice and considers him a mercy seat for reconciliation (Rom 3:25; cf. Exod 25). Jesus's faithfulness and his sacrifice should be understood together. That is, the former leads to the latter. Because he challenged the wisdom of the world, he was crucified. He was faithful to God and demonstrated God's righteousness. Now God's righteousness coming through Jesus's faithfulness is effective for all who have faith. This means those who participate in Jesus's faithfulness will be set right with God and called children of God: "The one who is righteous will live by faith" (Rom 1:17; Hab 2:4). As children of God, they must bring the gospel of God to all. They are a letter of Christ (2 Cor 3:3) and "ambassadors for Christ" (2 Cor 5:20). The gospel is not knowledge or teaching. It is the power of God for salvation. We need to communicate God's power through our word, deed, and involvement in the world. Different people may need different aspects of God's power: hope, empowerment, justice, and peace.

This book represents the best of my scholarship on Paul. I have studied and taught Paul for many years. I admire Paul not because he was a perfect theologian, apostle, or missionary but because he lived his best given his life situation, investing everything in his gospel proclamation. He was a critical, faithful thinker who worked hard to share the good news of God through the way of Christ. I hope this book will be a good resource for the study of Paul and his letters. After this introductory chapter, we will have two preliminary chapters: "An Overview of Paul" (chapter 1) and "An Overview of Paul's Letters" (chapter 2). Then we will revisit some familiar topics

---

18. Paul's apostolic call is set apart for "the gospel of God," as he says in Rom 1:1–2: "Paul, . . . set apart for the gospel of God, which he [God] promised beforehand through his prophets in the holy scriptures" (brackets in the original).

on Paul: the gospel (good news), righteousness/justification, faithfulness, freedom, new life / new creation, the body of Christ, the Holy Spirit.[19] We will analyze each theme/topic carefully in view of Paul's gospel. Each chapter involves the Greco-Roman and Jewish texts and contexts so that readers may understand the social, cultural, religious backdrop of Paul's thinking. Chapters 2–9 also include a summary section so that readers can review and reflect on the chapter's content. At the end of chapters 3–9, there is a "Questions for Reflection" section, which may be used for personal or group study.

19. For a discussion of key theological concepts in Paul's letters, see Jouette M. Bassler, *Navigating Paul: An Introduction to Key Theological Concepts* (Louisville: Westminster John Knox, 2007). She covers the topics as follows: "grace, the law, faith, 'in Christ,' 'the righteousness of God,' Israel, and Parousia." While her book touches on some important theological issues in Paul's letters, my book begins with "the gospel" and ends with "the Holy Spirit." In this way of reading Paul's letters, we can deal with the skeleton of his letters.

1

AN OVERVIEW OF PAUL

Paul was a Hellenistic Jew who believed that Jesus, the crucified one, is the Son of God and Messiah. He grew up as a
diasporic Jew, devoting himself to the study of the Torah.[1] He
was proud of his Jewish identity and religion. He was confident in himself, saying he was blameless "as to righteousness
under the law" (Phil 3:6).[2] But something happened to him
during his life that changed his view of God, the law, and the
Messiah. In this chapter, we will examine what caused him
to change his religious conviction and the reasons for his
radical change and will explore what he was trying to do in
his new vocation.

1. For more about Paul's life, see E. P. Sanders, *Paul: The Apostle's Life, Letters, and Thought*
(Minneapolis: Fortress, 2015), 3–82. See also Roetzel, *Letters of Paul*, 7–68.

2. Krister Stendahl, "The Apostle Paul and the Introspective Conscience of the West," *Harvard Theological Review* 56, no. 3 (1963): 199–215. Stendahl's view of Paul made a monumen-
tal impact on Pauline scholarship. Before him, by and large, Paul was understood from the
so-called old perspective on Paul. In this view, Judaism in the first century is considered a legalistic religion in that people keep the law to be justified. This kind of religion is called works-
righteousness. That is, they have to earn God's favor by doing great works. In this view, Paul
rejected his religion of the law because people cannot keep the law perfectly. Instead, he found
a new means of salvation or justification, which is faith—that is, Jesus's vicarious atonement
deals with sins. Those who believe that Jesus died for them are justified once and for all. This
view of justification is called "the forensic salvation" that God as a judge declares sinners are
innocent or righteous because of Jesus's vicarious death. The emphasis is justification by faith,
not by the law or works. This view on Judaism and Paul has been held for almost two thousand
years. This long-standing view is challenged by the New Perspective on Paul.

WHO IS PAUL?

In Acts, Paul is described as an apostle endorsed by the Jerusalem church and led by the Holy Spirit. Many of the key events in his life took place in and around Damascus (Acts 9:2–27; 22:5–11; Gal 1:17). In Acts 22:25–29, he is called a Roman citizen, which is also doubtful, since Paul never reveals his citizenship information. He is seen as a friend of Rome and does not seem to challenge Rome. But outside of the claim made in Acts, we do not know whether he was a Roman citizen. Neither do we know when or where Paul was born. Usually, his birth is placed between 10 BCE and 10 CE. This means he is a contemporary of Jesus. Though he does not reveal his hometown, Acts says he is "a Jew, from Tarsus in Cilicia" (Acts 21:39; 22:3). Tarsus is an important educational city where Paul may have been taught at the feet of Gamaliel (Acts 22:3). But Paul himself is silent about his education or hometown. According to Phil 3:4–8, he grew up as a Jewish boy, "being circumcised on the eighth day, a member of the people of Israel, of the tribe of Benjamin, a Hebrew born of Hebrews." All this means he is a Jew from a renowned Jewish family in the Diaspora and that he takes pride in being a Jew. More than that, he was a Pharisee, which means he was a devout Jew, studying and practicing the Jewish laws thoroughly. He says he felt no blame or guilt about the law. He was satisfied with being a Pharisee, being passionate about the law and his God.[3] He also says his passion led him to persecute the church of God (Phil 3:6; 1 Cor 15:9). Likewise, in Gal 1:13–14, he says similar things: "You have heard, no doubt, of my earlier life in Judaism. I was violently persecuting the church of God and was trying to destroy it. I advanced in Judaism beyond many among my people of the same age, for I was far more zealous for the traditions of my ancestors."

Then in 34 CE, about four years after Jesus died, he says he received a revelation about Christ from God: "But when God, who had set me apart before I was born and called me

---

3. See Garry Wills, *What Paul Meant* (New York: Penguin, 2006). Wills plainly writes about Paul's life and his relationships with Jesus, Peter, women, Jews, and Rome.

through his grace, was pleased to reveal his Son to me, so that I might proclaim him among the gentiles, I did not confer with any human being" (Gal 1:15–16). Paul's experience of receiving a revelation from God is close to the call of a prophet in the Old Testament. He received a prophetic call from God that he had to proclaim Christ crucified among the gentiles (Gal 1:15–17; 1 Cor 2:2). We can infer that God explained the significance of Jesus's life and death. Paul previously thought that God was the God of Jews only. But now he believes that God is one for all people and that he is the God of both Jews and gentiles (Rom 3:29–30). With this revelation from God, Paul experienced the grace of Jesus. He thought previously that Jesus failed on the cross, but now he realizes that the death of Jesus is the price for demonstrating God's righteousness/ love (Rom 3:22). Whoever comes to God through Christ's faithfulness will be reconciled to God and set right with God (Rom 3:26). God justifies both Jews and gentiles on the same basis of faith (Rom 3:30). Now the Abrahamic covenant extends to all through faith.

But this does not mean the law is outdated or ineffective; rather, Paul says the law is holy and upheld (Rom 3:30; 7:12). He argues that Christ clarified the purpose of the law and fulfilled it, as he implies in Rom 10:4: "Christ is the *telos* of the law." *Telos* means "end" or "purpose." The point is not that Jesus ended the law but that he fulfilled the law, which is the love of God and the love of neighbor (Rom 13:8–10; Gal 5:14).[4] He showed to the world that God is love. He did this through his faithfulness. As a result, God's righteousness was manifested in the world (Rom 3:22). "God's righteousness" means God's saving activity or God's character of love and justice.[5] Through Jesus's act of righteousness, God's justice and love were revealed.

After receiving God's revelation of his Son, Paul did not go up to Jerusalem to be endorsed by the Jerusalem apostles.

---

4. Mark Reasoner, *Romans in Full Circle* (Louisville: Westminster John Knox, 2005), 113–19.

5. Ernst Käsemann, *New Testament Questions of Today* (Philadelphia: Fortress, 1969), 168–82.

According to Acts 9:26–30, he went to Jerusalem after his conversion. But according to Gal 1:16–17, he went away into Arabia for some time and then returned to Damascus. Arabia is probably the Nabatean kingdom south of Damascus. We do not know why he went there or why he stayed for three years. He probably proclaimed the good news of God to people there and learned further about the gospel of Christ.

In 37 CE, he visited Jerusalem for the first time and briefly met Peter and James, the brother of Jesus. It was not a formal council meeting, which happened fourteen years later. He went again to Jerusalem to attend the Jerusalem Council in 51 CE. After this meeting, he continued on his mission to work in Galatia and Macedonia. In Ephesus, he prepared a final trip to Jerusalem to deliver the collection to the poor saints there. In Romans, his final letter, Paul expresses his intention to go to Jerusalem to deliver the collection, asking his readers to pray for his safe trip (Rom 15:25–26). According to Acts, he made one last trip to Jerusalem but was arrested and taken to Rome for trial. He was under house arrest in Rome. This period falls in about 59–62 CE. Then in 64 CE, he was probably martyred under Nero, as 1 Clem. 6:1 reports. We do not know whether Paul reached Spain for his intended final missionary journey. Acts does not report anything about Paul's death or his trip to Spain.

PAUL AS A PRACTICAL THEOLOGIAN

Paul was not a systematic, doctrinal theologian who was interested in formulating systematic theology for later churches or schools. Even as a Pharisee, he was not a quiet scholar of the Torah. When he heard Christians talking about the God of Jews, he could not sit idle watching his God be blasphemed by them. So passionate were his Jewish religious convictions that he persecuted the Christians. This core feature of Paul's personality remains with him after he received his revelation from God. After his conversion to Christianity, he engages with the world in a different but no less passionate way—proclaiming the gospel of God to the gentiles and claiming Jesus crucified is the Messiah.

His message is rooted in the good news that God is a liberator who chose the weak and despised (1 Cor 1:26–28). Paul's view of God is different from that of the Stoics who conceptualize God as an abstract idea and emphasize the unity of society. While their ideology seeks to form a unified, hierarchical community in which Zeus is the most supreme god, Paul's vision is to form a radical community of love, as he says in 1 Cor 1:25–30:

> For God's foolishness is wiser than human wisdom, and God's weakness is stronger than human strength. Consider your own call, brothers and sisters: not many of you were wise by human standards, not many were powerful, not many were of noble birth. But God chose what is foolish in the world to shame the wise; God chose what is weak in the world to shame the strong; God chose what is low and despised in the world, things that are not, to reduce to nothing things that are, so that no one might boast in the presence of God. He is the source of your life in Christ Jesus, who became for us wisdom from God, and righteousness and sanctification and redemption.

In this passage, Paul contrasts the wisdom of the world with the wisdom of God and the power of the world with the strength of God. God does not side with the elite and powerful in the world because they do not take care of the marginalized. God's foolishness or God's weakness presents a paradoxical truth that God takes care of those who are nobodies in society. In the Stoic vision of the world, the strong and the wise are taken care of, and they are the foundation of society. But in Paul's alternative world, God chooses the foolish and the weak. First Cor 1:25–30 is one of the most radical expressions of this theology.[6]

Paul's practical theology is also seen in his view of Jesus. He argues that God's love or righteousness was demonstrated

---

6. Alain Badiou, *Saint Paul: The Foundation of Universalism* (Stanford, CA: Stanford University Press, 2003).

by Jesus, "who became for us wisdom from God, and righteousness and sanctification and redemption" (1 Cor 1:30). God's love is not an abstract idea but was revealed through Christ's life and death. Jesus gave his life advocating for the weak and the despised. He deconstructed the wisdom of the world with the wisdom of God. In the eyes of the elites, Jesus was foolish or weak because he did not seek his power or wealth. But he was strong because he sought God's strength. Inspired by Christ's foolishness, Paul takes the role of being a fool in Christ.[7]

Paul's practical theology involves life-changing experiences of spiritual empowerment for everyday people who need freedom from sin and oppression. He persuades people not "with lofty words or wisdom . . . but with a demonstration of the Spirit of power," as he says to the Corinthians: "When I came to you, brothers and sisters, I did not come proclaiming the mystery of God to you in lofty words or wisdom. For I decided to know nothing among you except Jesus Christ, and him crucified. And I came to you in weakness and in fear and in much trembling. My speech and my proclamation were not with plausible words of wisdom, but with a demonstration of the Spirit and of power, so that your faith might rest not on human wisdom but on the power of God" (1 Cor 2:1–5). He proclaimed the gospel of Christ to the Corinthians so that they may live a new life of the Spirit and of power. He wanted them to experience a new life by the power of God. He also told them that "if anyone is in Christ, there is a new creation; everything old has passed away; see, everything has become new!" (2 Cor 5:17).

Paul's practical theology entails Christian ethics and participation in Christ. As followers of Jesus, Christians now have a new vocation as "ambassadors for Christ" (2 Cor 5:20). Mere belief in Jesus is not enough. *Christian* means those who

---

7. Laurence Welborn argues in his study of 1 Cor 1–4 that Paul takes the role of "the fool of Christ" for manifesting God's wisdom and power. See Laurence L. Welborn, *Paul, the Fool of Christ: A Study of 1 Corinthians 1–4 in the Comic-Philosophic Tradition* (New York: T&T Clark, 2005), 1–33.

follow Jesus and live by his faithfulness: those who die with him and live to God. To die with Jesus means to put to death the deeds of the body or sinful passion by the Spirit (Rom 8:13). Christians should make every effort to live holy in sanctification and spread the good news of God to all. They are free in Christ because they participate in Christ. If they follow the way of Christ, they will not be defeated by sin. They will serve as "instruments of righteousness," as Paul says in Rom 6:13: "No longer present your members to sin as instruments of wickedness, but present yourselves to God as those who have been brought from death to life, and present your members to God as instruments of righteousness."

As we saw previously, Paul's practical theology is based on his experience with God's love and Jesus's grace. The truth of the gospel is that God's good news or God's righteousness has been manifested through his Son, Jesus. Now all people may know and experience the love of God through Jesus. Paul's theology is God centered, Christ exemplified, and Christian imitated. So in Gal 2:20, Paul says Christ is everything for him and that he wants to live by his faith (Christ's faith): "It is no longer I who live, but it is Christ who lives in me. And the life I now live in the flesh I live by *the faith of the Son of God*, who loved me and gave himself for me" (italics indicate my translation, which emphasizes Christ's faithfulness).

As a practical theologian, Paul interprets the Scriptures as a story of faith from Abraham's faith to Jesus's. God called Abraham out of nowhere and blessed him and made a covenant with him. God also promised him that the whole world will be blessed in him (Gen 12:1–3; Gal 3). This promise of God was fulfilled and confirmed through Christ's faithfulness. All who follow Jesus and his faithfulness will be blessed and become children of God.

As a practical theologian, Paul responds to those who doubt the resurrection of the dead, and he reaffirms the power of God. Greek philosophy says resurrection is an impossible idea, since the body is rotten and only the soul is immortal. Paul knows this philosophy well and does not disagree with it. He does not say that the earthly body comes back on the last day. The resurrection body is "a spiritual body," which is an oxymoron to Hellenistic thinkers. While he does not explain what that body is, his point is clear that there is a resurrection of *the dead*. God has the power to resurrect them. "A spiritual body" is not a scientific statement but Paul's theological conviction that God cares for humanity, even after death. His point is that we have to trust God and that our faith rests not on ourselves but on God.

As a practical theologian, Paul is confident in his work and yet knows that he is weak. He claims that he is weak and that therefore he is strong (2 Cor 12:9–11). He asserts that he is "the least of the apostles, unfit to be called an apostle" because he persecuted the church of God (1 Cor 15:9). Though his words sound like a rhetorical gesture to appeal to the Corinthians, there is authenticity in them. He remembers who he was and how violently he behaved toward others who were not part of his faction. He goes on to say in 1 Cor 15:10, "By the grace of God I am what I am, and his grace toward me has not been in vain. On the contrary, I worked harder than any of them—though it was not I, but the grace of God that is with me." Paul was neither a perfect man nor a perfect apostle. Sometimes, he is very emotionally charged and upset, as in Galatians. At other times, he is calm and confident and able to deal with both theological and practical issues, like food offered to idols or the nature of marriage (1 Cor 8–11).

PAUL AS A MISSIONARY

When he received a new revelation from God, Paul says he did not go to Jerusalem immediately to be endorsed by the Jerusalem apostles but went away into Arabia for some time before returning to Damascus (Gal 1:16–17). While we do not know why he went to Arabia, it seems that he went there to proclaim the good news to its people, including those in the cities of the Decapolis. Then he returned to Damascus and went to Jerusalem. This was a courtesy visit. Then, sometime later, he went on his missionary journeys. According to Acts, he had three journeys, covering Asia Minor and Europe (Acts 13; 16; 19).

On his mission trips, Paul does not stay long in any one place and quickly leaves for another. He does not have enough time to ensure the vitality of the inchoate house church he established. If there are serious local issues, he receives a report from the local church members. Then he responds to them in writing.[8] First Corinthians is a good example of this dynamic. The letter is his response to various issues raised by the Corinthian leaders. At other times, he is very anxious about the members of the assembly he left behind, so he sends Timothy back to them to see how they are doing.

As a missionary to the gentiles, Paul was eager to proclaim the gospel of God in major cities of the Roman Empire (Rom 15:6). His message is consistent: God's righteousness was revealed through Christ. All those who participate in Christ will be free from the present evil age and will ultimately inherit eternal life. His gospel affirms the love of God, the grace of Jesus, and Christians' participation in that love and grace. His proclamation offers an alternative vision of community, filled with love, peace, and justice. Nevertheless, he knows his gospel will cause some trouble for the gentile members because gathering in the name of Jesus may be misunderstood by other gentiles. It remains unclear whether Paul required believers to abstain completely from participating in all social gatherings of surrounding polytheistic society (see, e.g., 1 Cor 8:1–13; 10:14–22). But Paul makes sure that Christians will not be misunderstood by the authorities and asks his readers to show good conduct toward them.

While the apostles in Jerusalem work for the salvation of Jews, Paul is devoted to the ministry for the gentiles. In Rom

8. Even though Paul neither visited Rome nor planted churches there, he knew the situation of the Roman house churches. He possibly gained the information about Rome through Priscilla and Aquila, a Jewish couple who were expelled from Rome because of the edict of Claudius and stayed in Corinth (Acts 18). Romans is close to an ambassadorial letter through which Paul wants to receive support from the Roman churches when he makes an eventual mission trip to Spain, which is considered the most marginalized place from the perspective of Rome.

15:15–16, he writes to the Roman Christians and states the purpose of his mission: "Nevertheless on some points I have written to you rather boldly by way of reminder, because of the grace given me by God to be a minister of Christ Jesus to the gentiles in the priestly service of the gospel of God, so that the offering of the gentiles may be acceptable, sanctified by the Holy Spirit." These verses echo Gal 1:15–16, where Paul talks about God's special call for the gentiles. He, as a minister of Christ to the gentiles, serves a purpose of proclaiming the gospel of God to them, which will lead to an acceptable, pleasing offering to God. Paul thinks his job is like that of a priest who takes the offering to God. He can do this job as a minister of Christ, through the gospel of Christ, who gave himself for humanity. In Phil 3:7–9, he is determined to proclaim this good news of Christ: "Yet whatever gains I had, these I have come to regard as loss because of Christ. More than that, I regard everything as loss because of the surpassing value of knowing Christ Jesus my Lord. For his sake I have suffered the loss of all things, and I regard them as rubbish, in order that I may gain Christ and be found in him, not having a righteousness of my own that comes from the law, but one that comes *through the faithfulness of Christ*, the righteousness from God based on faith."

PAUL AS A COMMUNITY ORGANIZER

In general, the Pauline house churches were small. The Corinthian house church had about thirty to forty members. But even in this small gathering, there are issues that need attention from Paul himself. When four factions arise in the Corinthian church (1 Cor 1:12), his advice is to imitate Christ, who is the foundation of the church (1 Cor 3:11). Paul knows what is foundational for the church. It is not knowledge, spiritual gifts, money, or persons. The foundation is Christ, his grace, and his sacrifice. The foundation of the church is not merely Jesus's death but his grace, his love, and his faithfulness. In Paul's theology, Jesus's death is understood variously. It may be understood as the result of his faithful obedience to the will of God, which is a demonstration of God's righteousness/ love in the world. In other words, Jesus's death is the result of his challenge to the system that resists God's righteousness. It may also be understood as the result of Christ's love that he did not give up on his mission for God's righteousness. While we will explore more about Jesus's faithfulness in the main chapters of this book, suffice it to say that Paul's community philosophy is rooted in the way of Christ: his life-giving spirit and faithfulness to God's will.

When Paul refers to the church, he uses the phrase "the church of God" (Gal 1:13; 1 Cor 1:2; 10:32; 15:9; 2 Cor 1:1), not "the church of Christ." Paul seems to distinguish between the foundation of the church, which is Christ, and the owner of the church, who is God (1 Cor 3:11). The church should be built on the love of Christ (1 Cor 13:1–13). Love builds up! (1 Cor 8:1). Members of the church have to see Christ's sacrifice, his faith, and his love for the church and the world. Whatever they do in the church, they must show the love of Christ. They must honor one another, taking care of the weak members, being united with the spirit of Christ. They are one, not because they think in uniform terms, but because they are united with the mind of Christ, who resembles love, sacrifice, and faith.[9]

In Paul's community, all are taken care of equally. There is no head in the body of Christ (1 Cor 12:12–27). The hierarchical body metaphor appears only in the disputable letters of Paul—for example, in Col 1:18: "He is the head of the body, the church; he is the beginning, the firstborn from the dead, so that he might come to have first place in everything" (cf. Col 1:24; Eph 1:22–23; 4:1; 5:23). In these later letters, the author states clearly that Christ is the head of the church. But in 1 Cor 12:12–27 or in Rom 12:4–5, Paul does not talk about the church's head. Rather, all members constitute the body, the church, or Christ's body. All are taken care of and all work together. They rejoice and suffer together. They are

9. For a full discussion about "the body of Christ" as a metaphor and members' participation in Christ, see chapter 9 in this book.

in solidarity with each other. All members (from head to feet) are united to Christ.[10]

As a community organizer, Paul leads an exemplary life. In Thessalonica, he works night and day with his hands so as not to financially burden the members of the church with supporting him. On his mission journey, he does not receive financial gifts from the members of the local church where he is working. And throughout his ministry, he is wary about the rich's influence on his gospel.

As a community organizer, Paul is different from Jesus. Paul is a follower and organizer of the Jesus movement, while Jesus is the movement's founder. As a founder, Jesus was free to act boldly against the norms of society. He ate with sinners and tax collectors. He broke boundaries between the sacred and the profane. He was an idealistic visionary who believed that God's reign is possible in the here and now.[11] In the parable of "the wheat and weeds" (Matt 13:24–30), Jesus talks about the master representing an idealistic realist who does not want to remove "bad" things from the world because he hopes for the transformation of all. Given the reality that good and evil are intertwined in the world, it is hard to separate good from bad. Even a good person may be evil inside, and even an evil person may not be forever evil. This parable seems to contain Jesus's thinking about the world. His point is that we should not judge people on the basis of the current reality.

While Paul's message is as radical as Jesus's in terms of God's righteousness, he is a follower of Jesus who is concerned about maintaining community. He is a realistic perfectionist who strives to ensure the health of the community. He advises the offender to be expelled from the community (1 Cor 5:1–8). He is cautious about society, which might threaten his community.

10. See Yung Suk Kim, "Reclaiming Christ's Body (*soma christou*): Embodiment of God's Gospel in Paul's Letters," *Interpretation* 67, no. 1 (2013): 20–29. See also Robert Jewett, *Paul, the Apostle to America: Cultural Trends and Pauline Scholarship* (Louisville: Westminster John Knox, 1994), 3–69.

11. See Yung Suk Kim, *Jesus's Truth: Life in Parables* (Eugene, OR: Resource, 2018), 47–50.

He asks the members of the community to show good conduct to people in the world so that they may not be misunderstood by them. He asks the members to cooperate with the governing authorities, doing their civic duties, such as paying taxes and working diligently. Paul's advice is based on his apocalyptic thinking that in the end, God will intervene in the world. He lives between the times, following Jesus while trying to protect the Jesus movement from harm.

2

AN OVERVIEW OF PAUL'S LETTERS

There are many differences between Paul's undisputed letters and the Deutero-Pauline and Pastoral letters.[1] The differences have to do with the writing style, vocabulary, theological views, and the issues being addressed.[2] By comparing and contrasting Paul's undisputed letters with the other letters, we can discern the authentic teachings of Paul and his practical theology. We will ask why he was so eager to proclaim the gospel, what the content of his gospel was, and what he wanted to achieve through his mission work. These questions are important because, as we saw in the previous chapter, Paul is a practical theologian, missionary, and community organizer who is passionate about his gospel for the gentiles.

1. Yung Suk Kim, A *Theological Introduction to Paul's Letters: Exploring a Threefold Theology of Paul* (Eugene, OR: Cascade, 2011), 38–108. See also Leander E. Keck, *Christ's First Theologian: The Shape of Paul's Thought* (Waco, TX: Baylor University Press, 2015), 3–28. See also John Dominic Crossan and Marcus Borg, *The First Paul: Reclaiming the Radical Visionary behind the Church's Conservative Icon* (New York: HarperCollins, 2010).

2. See Mitzi Smith and Yung Suk Kim, *Toward Decentering the New Testament: A Reintroduction* (Eugene, OR: Cascade, 2018), 195–292.

THE UNDISPUTED LETTERS VS. THE DEUTERO-PAULINE AND PASTORAL LETTERS

Traditionally, all thirteen letters with Paul's name were attributed to him. But critical scholarship breaks them into three categories: Paul's seven undisputed letters, the Deutero-Pauline letters, and the Pastoral letters. Paul's authorship is not questioned in regard to these seven letters: 1 Thessalonians, Galatians, Philippians, 1 Corinthians, 2 Corinthians, Philemon, and Romans. While the Pauline authorship of the Deutero-Pauline letters (Col, Eph, and 2 Thess) is debatable, that of the Pastoral letters (1 Tim, 2 Tim, and Titus) is rejected by the overwhelming majority. As such, these are non-Pauline letters.[3] In the following, we will examine various theological differences between Paul's undisputed letters and the post-Pauline letters.

CENTER OF PAUL'S PRACTICAL THEOLOGY

Eschatology

Paul's undisputed letters present an imminent eschatology in which Paul announces that the Lord would come back soon and that salvation will be completed in the future while Christians may live a new life in Christ now. They also have to fight against evil in the world until the Parousia. In 1 Thess 5:1–11, Paul states this view of the last time:

> Now concerning the times and the seasons, brothers and sisters, you do not need to have anything written to you. For you yourselves know very well that the day of the Lord will come like a thief in the night. When they say, "There is peace and security,"

3. Pseudepigrapha is a type of literature that flourished from the second century BCE to the first century CE in Jewish land. Authors of this literature write in somebody else's name, such as Enoch or Abraham, to appeal to more people. Pseudepigrapha should not be thought of as a forgery from a modern perspective because in ancient culture, sometimes, pupils of a great teacher write in the name of their teacher. It is a kind of accepted practice. Possibly, Paul's students thought they were continuing their teacher and wrote some letters. See Smith and Kim, *Toward Decentering the New Testament*, 287.

then sudden destruction will come upon them, as labor pains come upon a pregnant woman, and there will be no escape! But you, beloved, are not in darkness, for that day to surprise you like a thief; for you are all children of light and children of the day; we are not of the night or of darkness. So then let us not fall asleep as others do, but let us keep awake and be sober; for those who sleep sleep at night, and those who are drunk get drunk at night. But since we belong to the day, let us be sober, and put on the breastplate of faith and love, and for a helmet the hope of salvation. For God has destined us not for wrath but for obtaining salvation through our Lord Jesus Christ, who died for us, so that whether we are awake or asleep we may live with him. Therefore encourage one another and build up each other, as indeed you are doing.

Similarly, Paul speaks to the Corinthians in 1 Cor 7:29–31: "I mean, brothers and sisters, the appointed time has grown short; from now on, let even those who have wives be as though they had none, and those who mourn as though they were not mourning, and those who rejoice as though they were not rejoicing, and those who buy as though they had no possessions, and those who deal with the world as though they had no dealings with it. For the present form of this world is passing away."

In contrast, the Deutero-Pauline and Pastoral letters do not emphasize imminent eschatology. Rather, their emphasis is on God's complete salvation in the present: God "has rescued us from the power of darkness and transferred us into the kingdom of his beloved Son" (Col 1:13; also, 2:8–15; 3:1–4). There is less emphasis on the last day. For example, in 2 Thess 2:2–12, the author says the last day will not come as soon as people expect and that there will be some sign before that day. The author writes, "The rebellion comes first and the lawless one is revealed, the one destined for destruction" (2 Thess 2:3). Similarly, in 1 Tim 4:1–5, we see the author's caution for people who forbid marriage and demand of others an ascetic lifestyle. The author argues that food is good and that all things God created are good. The implication is that

Christians should not think that the end will come soon and that this world is a good creation of God in which they can live a good life in Christ as children of God.

Salvation

In Paul's undisputed letters, salvation is completed in the future, on the last day. Until then, followers of Jesus have to participate in Christ through faith and strive for sanctification (Rom 5:1; 6:4; Gal 6:14–15; 2 Cor 5:17). While they may live a new life in Christ today, their complete salvation is yet to come. This view is observed throughout 1 Thessalonians, 1 Corinthians 15, and Romans. For example, in Rom 6:5, Paul writes, "For if we have been united with him in a death like his, we will certainly be united with him in a resurrection like his." Salvation is understood as full recovery of God's creation (Rom 8:19–25) and as deliverance from the power of sin (Rom 6:14; 7:21–25; 8:2–4).

But in the Deutero-Pauline letters such as Ephesians and Colossians, salvation is expressed in the past tense (Eph 2:5–8; Col 1:13; 2:12–13; 3:1). For example, Eph 2:5–8 reads as follows: "Even when we were dead through our trespasses, made us alive together with Christ—by grace you *have been saved*—and *raised us up with him and seated us with him in the heavenly places in Christ Jesus,* so that in the ages to come he might show the immeasurable riches of his grace in kindness toward us in Christ Jesus. For by grace you *have been saved through faith*, and this is not your own doing; it is the gift of God" (italics mine). Likewise, the post-Pauline letters emphasize the completion of salvation and the forgiveness of sins through the blood of Jesus. For example, Eph 1:7 reads, "In him we have redemption through his blood, the forgiveness of our trespasses" (similarly, "the blood of his cross" in Col 1:20; cf. Col 2:13). It is important to note that in his undisputed letters, Paul never uses phrases like "the forgiveness of sins" or "the blood of Jesus." Instead, he emphasizes Christ's death or Christ crucified, phrases and concepts that have to do with the demonstration of God's love or righteousness. For Paul, Christ crucified is the central topic of his proclamation, as he says, "We proclaim Christ crucified" (1 Cor 1:23); "For I decided to know nothing among you except Jesus Christ, and him crucified" (1 Cor 2:2). The meaning of Christ crucified has to do with Christ's love of God and God's people. That is, Christ was crucified because he advocated for the weak and challenged the system that victimized them. In this way, he demonstrated God's righteousness or God's love to the world.

Christology

In the undisputed letters, Paul characterizes Jesus as the Son of God, who is faithful to God and yields to God on the last day (1 Cor 15:23). Christ's faithfulness is seen in Gal 2:16, 20; Rom 3:22; and Phil 3:8. Christ's death is the result of his faithfulness in demonstrating God's righteousness. But in the post-Pauline letters, the author articulates a high Christology, seeing Christ as a triumphant Savior. He is "the image of the invisible God" (Col 1:15) and "the head over all things for the church" (Eph 1:22). He is also "the head of the church" (Col 1:18; Eph 1:22–23; 4:1; 5:23). In the undisputed letters, Paul considers Jesus not as the head of the church but rather as its foundation: "For no one can lay any foundation other than the one that has been laid; that foundation is Jesus Christ" (1 Cor 3:11). All members of the church are respected and united with Christ (1 Cor 12:12–27; 6:12–20).

Faith

In Paul's undisputed letters, he emphasizes both Christ's faithfulness and Christians' faithfulness. A significant scholarly debate exists over the meaning of *pistis christou* (faith of Christ) in Rom 3:21–26 and Gal 2:16–21, and this is discussed more in-depth in later chapters. For Paul, faith means trust, loyalty, and participation in God's grace.[4] So followers of Jesus must imitate Christ, dying with him, dying to sin, living to God (Rom 6). Paul also emphasizes God's faithfulness in 1 Cor 1:9: "God is faithful; by him you

---

4. See Yung Suk Kim, *Preaching the New Testament Again: Faith, Freedom, and Transformation* (Eugene, OR: Cascade, 2018), 8–36.

were called into the fellowship of his Son, Jesus Christ our Lord." But in the Deutero-Pauline and Pastoral letters, the concept of faith changes. Faith means salvific knowledge or teaching about Jesus (Eph 1:15; 2:8–9; 3:12, 17; 4:5, 13; 1 Tim 1:3–5; 4:6; 2 Tim 1:13). Jesus Christ is the object of faith, and his own faith is not discussed in these letters. We see instead the form "faith in Christ" (*pistis en christo*), a phrase indicating that Christ is only the object of faith (Col 1:4; 1 Tim 3:13; 2 Tim 1:13; 3:15). The other big difference between Paul's undisputed letters and the Pastoral letters has to do with the separation between faith and works. For Paul, faith includes the notion of good works (Gal 5:6: "faith working through love"). But in the Pastoral letters, faith and good works are separate, and the former needs the latter (1 Tim 2:10; 5:10; 6:8; 2 Tim 2:21; Titus 2:14). And as another New Testament writer, James, makes clear, faith without work is dead (Jas 2:14–26).

Women

Paul affirms the place of women in the church. He had women coworkers as leaders of the church (Phoebe, Priscilla, Junia).[5] Women are gifted with the Spirit and freely participate in worship (1 Cor 11:5), prophesying and speaking in tongues (1 Cor 12–14). An outlier passage, 1 Cor 14:33b–36, is considered to be an interpolation because this passage is incongruous with Paul's other undisputed letters. This passage is similar to 1 Tim 2:11–15, which is non-Pauline. That is why scholars believe that 1 Cor 14:33b–36 was inserted by a later copyist. In 1 Tim 2:11–15, which reflects post-Pauline churches, women are prohibited from teaching in the church. This prohibition is found in the "household codes" (Eph 5:22–6:9; Col 3:18–4:1). As Eve is singled out as a seed of evil, so women as a whole are viewed similarly. As 1 Tim 2:11–15 states, "Let

---

5. See Bernadette Brooten, "Junia—Outstanding among the Apostles (Romans 6:7)," in *Women Priests: A Catholic Commentary on the Vatican Declaration*, ed. J. Leonard and Arlene Swidler (New York: Paulist, 1977), 141–44. See also Eldon Epp, *Junia: The First Woman Apostle* (Minneapolis: Fortress, 2005).

a woman learn in silence with full submission. I permit no woman to teach or to have authority over a man; she is to keep silent. For Adam was formed first, then Eve; and Adam was not deceived, but the woman was deceived and became a transgressor. Yet she will be saved through childbearing, provided they continue in faith and love and holiness, with modesty."

Marriage

Paul's view of marriage is nuanced. Basically, his advice to followers of Jesus is not to marry if they can because the end of time is near. Otherwise, marriage is not forbidden. If they can, they should stay celibate because it allows them to devote themselves to God (1 Cor 7:7–8, 36–38). Spousal relations are interdependent (1 Cor 7). But in the Pastoral letters, marriage is encouraged (1 Tim 5:14), and spousal relationships are hierarchical, as stated in the household codes.

Politics

Paul's political view is nuanced. He is neither a revolutionary nor a pacifist nor a conformist to imperial ideology. His politics or ethics are limited by his belief that the world is soon to end. Until then, he does his best to demonstrate and encourage good conduct in society. But he does not attempt to abolish the evil systems in society like slavery. Nevertheless, he implicitly challenges the Roman system when he says, "You were bought with a price; do not become slaves of human masters" (1 Cor 7:23). He alludes to the Roman Empire when he talks about the Roman slogan of "peace and security" in 1 Thess 5:3: "When they say, 'There is peace and security,' then sudden destruction will come upon them, as labor pains come upon a pregnant woman, and there will be no escape!" Paul also says in 1 Cor 1:27–28, "But God chose what is foolish in the world to shame the wise; God chose what is weak in the world to shame the strong; God chose what is low and despised in the world, things that are not, to reduce to nothing things that are." Furthermore, Rom 13:1–7 should not be read as blind obedience to the government. Rather, we need to consider the probable context of this passage. Paul's warning is to those who are not working or paying taxes to the governing authorities. In the household codes of the Deutero-Pauline and Pastoral letters, by contrast, rigid hierarchy is imposed on the community, one that accepts the prevailing conventions of society. For example, 1 Tim 6:1 reads, "Let all who are under the yoke of slavery regard their masters as worthy of all honor, so that the name of God and the teaching may not be blasphemed" (cf. Titus 3:1).

Ecclesiology

For Paul, *ekklesia* ("gathering" or "church") is egalitarian (Gal 3:28; 1 Cor 12:12–27). The church belongs to God ("the church of God" in Gal 1:13; 1 Cor 1:2; 10:32; 11:32; 15:9; 2 Cor 1:1), and its foundation is Christ (1 Cor 3:11). Contrary to popular understanding, Paul does not equate "the body of Christ" with the church. Even though he says in 1 Cor 12:27, "You are the body of Christ," what he says here is "you" (not the church) constitute "the body of Christ," which may be a community or Christ's own body in a different sense. The idea that the church is the body of Christ appears in Col 1:18: "He is *the head of the body, the church*; he is the beginning, the firstborn from the dead, so that he might come to have first place in everything" (italics mine). Here, the "body" is used as a metaphor, as also seen in Eph 4:12: "building up the body of Christ." In later churches after Paul, the egalitarian community becomes a hierarchical one (as reflected in the household codes). The church as the body of Christ defends the deposit of faith (1 Tim 6:20; 2 Tim 1:12, 14) and is the "pillar and bulwark of the truth" (1 Tim 3:15). Likewise, the church leaders must protect sound teaching (1 Tim 6:20; 2 Tim 1:12, 14).

God

For Paul, God is the beginning and end. God created the world and humanity and blessed Abraham. God promised the good news "through his prophets in the holy scriptures" (Rom 1:2). God's promise is that all people will be blessed in Abraham's faith. God sent his Son, Jesus, who fulfilled God's promise through faithfulness. God justifies the one who has the faithfulness of Jesus (Rom 3:26). The Holy Spirit or the Spirit also works with God, comforting and empowering his children so that they may continue to stay in the love of God in Christ. At the end of time, Jesus completes his salvific vocation: "Then comes the end, when he hands over the kingdom to God the Father, after he has destroyed every ruler and every authority and power" (1 Cor 15:24). Until the end, God is faithful, loving, righteous. God sends the Spirit of Jesus into the hearts of his children. God participates in redeeming the world through Jesus and the Spirit.

But in the Deutero-Pauline and Pastoral letters, by contrast, we do not see this dynamic work of God in history. Rather, God is depicted as immortal, invisible (1 Tim 1:17), transcendent (Eph 1:4), and omniscient (Eph 1:9; Col 1:26). However, we do not know whether the absence of discussion about the active God proves that God is understood passively in these letters.

OVERVIEW OF PAUL'S UNDISPUTED LETTERS

Paul was eager to share the good news of God that now the gentiles can become children of God through faith. God's promise given to Abraham, which is the blessing of the gentiles, was fulfilled through Christ's faithfulness. Paul believes that Christ demonstrated God's righteousness through faithfulness (Rom 3:22). Jesus was crucified because he advocated for the weak and despised, as Paul implies in 1 Cor 1:18–25. Paul was deeply inspired by Jesus's grace that was shown in his crucifixion. So he decided to proclaim Christ crucified only (1 Cor 1:23; 2:2). During his missionary journey, Paul delivers the message about Christ, as he understands it. First Cor 1:18–25 shows Paul's message about Christ crucified and its relationship with the power of God and the wisdom of God:

> For the message about the cross is foolishness to those who are perishing, but to us who are being saved it is the power of God. For it is written, "I will destroy the wisdom of the wise, and

the discernment of the discerning I will thwart." Where is the one who is wise? Where is the scribe? Where is the debater of this age? Has not God made foolish the wisdom of the world? For since, in the wisdom of God, the world did not know God through wisdom, God decided, through the foolishness of our proclamation, to save those who believe. For Jews demand signs and Greeks desire wisdom, but we proclaim Christ crucified, a stumbling block to Jews and foolishness to gentiles, but to those who are the called, both Jews and Greeks, Christ the power of God and the wisdom of God. For God's foolishness is wiser than human wisdom, and God's weakness is stronger than human strength.

Living as he did in a world of injustices, we can ask how Paul could ignore the cries of voiceless people when talking about Christ crucified. How could he not see the broken, maimed bodies of the slaves in the Roman world when proclaiming the Christ who was killed on a Roman cross? For Paul, Jesus's crucifixion is an unjust tragedy. It is the torture of an innocent man. It is, thus, the wisdom of the world that killed Jesus. At the same time, the cross of Jesus shows his love and grace in that he did not spare his own life to demonstrate God's justice in the world. Paul's signature message is Christ crucified, which shows not only God's wisdom and power but also the way Christians must live. With this central message in mind, we will review Paul's undisputed letters.

Romans

Romans is the longest and last letter written by Paul. It was sent to the church in Rome, a church that he did not found. He never visited Rome, but he may have known some Jews expelled from Rome under the edict of Claudius in the late 40s. For example, Paul met Priscilla and Aquila who came from Rome and stayed in Corinth (Acts 18:1–18). Romans resembles an ambassadorial letter in which Paul aims to achieve several things. First, he wants to have fellowship in Christ with Roman Christians, strengthening their faith and sharing his passion for the gospel (Rom 1:8–15). Second, when he goes to Spain via Rome for his final mission trip, he hopes to receive their support. He expresses this hope clearly: "For I do hope to see you on my journey and to be sent on by you, once I have enjoyed your company for a little while" (Rom 15:24). Third, he wants to make sure there are no misunderstandings about his gospel. He summarizes his gospel in 1:1–17. The gospel is "the power of God for salvation to everyone who has faith" (Rom 1:16). The good news is not knowledge or doctrine. It comes from God, and it is about God. The gospel reveals "the righteousness of God," which means God's love and justice. Those who have faith can experience God's love. God wants his people to live by faith (Rom 1:17).

In part 1, 1:18–11:36, Paul explains his gospel of faith that does not reject the law or Israel. After pointing out the problem of human unfaithfulness in 1:18–3:20, he explains the solution to that problem in 3:21–4:25. God's righteousness has been revealed through Christ's faithfulness, and it is effective for all who have faith (Rom 3:22). Then, in 5:1–21, he talks about the "new life" that comes through Christ's act of righteousness. Those who follow Jesus will live a new life free from sinful passions. In 6:1–7:25, Paul talks about how to maintain this new life in Christ through dying to sin and the law. "Dying to sin" means not being defeated by sin. This happens when one puts to death the deeds of the body by the Spirit (Rom 8:13). "Dying to the law" means the law should not become a condition for justification. The law is holy, and yet it should not overwrite faith. Conversely, faith cannot overthrow the law.

In 8:1–39, Paul sums up the new life in Christ and asks Roman Christians to be led by the Spirit. In 9:1–29, he deals with the place of Israel in the drama of salvation. In 9:30–10:21, he argues that God's righteousness comes to Jews and gentiles through faith, not by the law. In 11:1–36, he talks about God's power and providence for his people. He hopes that God will save his people in the future. In part 2, 12:1–15:13, he talks about the gospel's power of transformation for the community and society. Then part 3,

15:14–16:27, deals with concluding matters such as his travel plans and greetings.

Outline of Romans

1:1–17 Prologue to Romans[6]

1:18–11:36 The Gospel of Faith That Does Not Reject the Law or Israel

1:18–3:20 The Problem of Unfaithfulness

3:21–4:25 Righteousness through Christ's Faithfulness

5:1–21 New Life through Christ's Act of Righteousness

6:1–7:25 Maintenance of New Life: Dying to Sin and Dying to the Law

8:1–39 New Life in the Spirit

9:1–29 The Dilemma of Israel in the Gospel of God

9:30–10:21 Righteousness for Jew and gentile through Faithfulness

11:1–36 The Mystery of Salvation of Israel

12:1–15:13 The Gospel's Power of Transformation

15:14–16:27 Concluding Matters

---

6. This outline is based on Kim, *Rereading Romans*, 4–105. For a thematic overview and literary, theological contents of Romans, see Luke T. Johnson, *Reading Romans: A Literary and Theological Commentary* (Macon, GA: Smyth & Helwys, 2013). For a short commentary on Romans, see Cynthia Briggs Kittredge, "Romans," in *The New Testament: Fortress Commentary on the Bible*, ed. Margaret Aymer, Cynthia Briggs Kittredge, and David A. Sanchez (Minneapolis: Fortress, 2014), 395–426. For a thorough commentary on Romans, see Robert Jewett, *Romans: A Commentary* (Minneapolis: Fortress, 2007). For a rhetorical reading of Romans, see Stanley Stowers, *A Rereading of Romans: Justice, Jews and Gentiles* (New Haven: Yale University Press, 1994). For various cultural readings of Romans, see K. K. Yeo, ed., *Navigating Romans through Cultures: Challenging Readings by Charting a New Course* (New York: T&T Clark, 2004). For a contextual reading of Romans, see Daniel Patte, "Romans," in the *Global Bible Commentary*, ed. Daniel Patte (Nashville: Abingdon, 2004), 429–43.

1 Corinthians

This letter responds to the immense problems among the believing community in Corinth, ranging from sexual immorality to community division to denial of the resurrection of Jesus. Paul writes this letter because he received a verbal report from Chloe's people as well as letters from the Corinthians concerning these and other issues: sexual immorality (1 Cor 5–6), questions about marriage and celibacy (1 Cor 7), food offered to idols (1 Cor 8–11), spiritual gifts (1 Cor 12–14), resurrection (1 Cor 15). In 1 Corinthians, Paul responds to these problems one by one.

In 1 Cor 1–4, he addresses community division, insisting that the Corinthians have to follow Christ's faith and his spirit. The foundation of the church is Christ (1 Cor 3:11). Christians, therefore, should not seek the strength and wisdom of the world that ignore the foolish, the weak, and the low. In response to the reports of sexual immorality, Paul writes, "'All things are lawful for me,' but not all things are beneficial. 'All things are lawful for me, but I will not be dominated by anything'" (1 Cor 6:12). Since their bodies are "parts" (melē) of Christ, they should not become "parts of a prostitute" (1 Cor 6:15). Paul says in 1 Cor 6:16, "Do you not know that whoever is united to a prostitute becomes one body with her?" Here "union with a prostitute" means to follow the way of a prostitute, while "parts of Christ" means they should be united with Christ by following the way of Christ. Union with Christ means "to become one spirit with him" (1 Cor 6:17). Paul's conclusion is at 1 Cor 6:20: "For you were bought with a price; therefore glorify God in your body."

Concerning marriage and celibacy, Paul's response is clear that celibacy is to be preferred over marriage or remarriage. The reason is simple: because the end of time is near, Christians should give their undivided devotion to God and God's work. Concerning food offered to idols, Paul's response is more delicate. People may participate in civic society or eat food offered to idols if their faith is strong because food itself is not unclean. But if there are some weak people who are influenced by this act, Paul's advice is not to eat it because they have to take care of one another. At the Lord's Supper, members should be careful about the union with Christ. They are one because they care for one another, as Paul talks about this in 1 Cor 12:12–27. Similarly, in 1 Cor 12–14, Paul deals with the issue of spiritual gifts. His advice is that individual Christians should build up the community and should not exercise gifts for edifying themselves by boasting about them. Ultimately, the most excellent gift is love (1 Cor 13). Finally, concerning the issue of resurrection, Paul affirms the resurrection of the dead because it is God's power. He concludes the letter by detailing his travel plans and making an appeal for monetary support for the Christians in Jerusalem.

Outline of 1 Corinthians

1:1–17 Paul, Apostle of Christ Jesus, and the Corinthians, Sanctified in Christ Jesus[7]

1:18–4:21 The Cross as God's Power, Exemplified by the Corinthians and Embodied by Paul

5:1–11:34 The Corinthians' Failure to Embody Christ Crucified; Paul's Exhortations to the Corinthians Calling for Participation in Christ Crucified

12:1–15:11 Exhortation: The Corinthian Body as Christic Embodiment

15:12–58 As Christ Crucified Was Raised, So the Crucified Body of Christians Will Be Raised

16:1–24 Conclusion

---

7. This outline is based on Kim, *Christ's Body in Corinth*, 72–73. See also Smith and Kim, *Toward Decentering the New Testament*, 221–35. For a short commentary on 1 Corinthians, see Laura S. Nasrallah, "1 Corinthians," in *New Testament: Fortress Commentary*, 427–71. For a full commentary on 1 Corinthians, see Joseph Fitzmyer, *First Corinthians: A New Translation with Introduction and Commentary* (New Haven: Yale University Press, 2008). See also Anthony Thieselton, *The First Epistle to the Corinthians* (Grand Rapids: Eerdmans, 2000). For an African American reading of 1 Corinthians, see Boykin Sanders, "1 Corinthians," in *True to Our Native Land*, 276–306. For a contextual reading of 1–2 Corinthians, see Yung Suk Kim, ed., *1 and 2 Corinthians: Texts at Contexts* (Minneapolis: Fortress, 2013).

2 Corinthians

According to scholarly consensus, 2 Corinthians is not a single letter but rather a composite letter.[8] It is composed of at least the four distinct correspondences: the letter of the collection (2 Cor 8), the letter of defense (2 Cor 2:14–7:4), the letter of tears (2 Cor 10–13), and the letter of reconciliation (2 Cor 1:1–2:13; 7:5–16; 13:11–13).

The letter of the collection (2 Cor 8) represents Paul's program of helping the poor saints at Jerusalem. In the letter of defense (2 Cor 2:14–7:4), Paul defends his ministry based on Christ's work. The ministry of Christ is not by words only but through the power of the Spirit (2 Cor 3:3). His good news is based not on the law but on the spirit of God. Jesus exemplified what the law requires: to love God and to love neighbors. That is a new covenant. If the laws were written on the tablets of stone, a "letter of Christ" is "written not with ink but with the Spirit of the living God, not on tablets of stone but on tablets of human hearts" (2 Cor 3:3). Christ exemplified God's love through his life and death, and therefore, the Corinthians must continue to carry this letter of Christ. They are a letter of Christ. No hardships or suffering will prevent Paul from living out the gospel of Christ.

As time went by, however, the Corinthian church did not improve, and the church's relationship with Paul deteriorated. He made a second visit to Corinth to try to remedy the situation, but his visit ended in public shame. He returned to Ephesus and penned a letter of tears, which is preserved in 2 Cor 10–13. In this emotionally charged letter, he acknowledges that he is weak and foolish (2 Cor 11:23–27) but argues that weakness is the source of power (2 Cor 11:30). He summarizes his philosophy of weakness in 2 Cor 12:8–11:

8. For example, see Brent Nongbri, "2 Corinthians and Possible Material Evidence for Composite Letters in Antiquity," in *Collecting Early Christian Letters: From the Apostle Paul to Late Antiquity*, ed. B. Neil and P. Allen (Cambridge: Cambridge University Press, 2015), 54–67. See also N. H. Taylor, "The Composition and Chronology of Second Corinthians," *Journal for the Study of the New Testament* 14, no. 44 (1991): 67–87.

Three times I appealed to the Lord about this, that it would leave me, but he said to me, "My grace is sufficient for you, for power is made perfect in weakness." So, I will boast all the more gladly of my weaknesses, so that the power of Christ may dwell in me. Therefore I am content with weaknesses, insults, hardships, persecutions, and calamities for the sake of Christ; for whenever I am weak, then I am strong. I have been a fool! You forced me to it. Indeed you should have been the ones commending me, for I am not at all inferior to these super-apostles, even though I am nothing.

Some time after the letter of tears was sent, the Corinthians repented, and the wrongdoer among them was punished. Paul then writes a letter of reconciliation, thanking them for their understanding. He asks the Corinthians to forgive the wrongdoer and extend their love to him. He also tries to solidify the church of God through God's mercy.

Outline of 2 Corinthians

2 Cor 8 Letter of the Collection[9]

2 Cor 2:14–7:4 Letter of Defense

2 Cor 10–13 Letter of Tears

2 Cor 1:1–2:13; 7:5–16; 13:11–13 Letter of Reconciliation

Galatians

Galatians was written to deal with the issue of the perversion of the gospel, as Paul says in Gal 1:6–7: "I am astonished that you are so quickly deserting the one who called you in the grace of Christ and are turning to a different gospel—not that there is another gospel, but there are some who are confusing you and want to pervert the gospel of Christ." Perversion

---

9. For a short commentary on 2 Corinthians, see David E. Fredrickson, "2 Corinthians," in *New Testament: Fortress Commentary*, 473–501. For a commentary on 2 Corinthians, see Victor Furnish, *2 Corinthians* (Garden City: Doubleday, 1984). See also Craig S. Keener, *1–2 Corinthians* (New York: Cambridge University Press, 2005).

of the gospel in this instance means that there are some Galatians who insist that the gentile Christians should be circumcised. They say faith is not enough and that the gentiles should follow Jewish custom and culture. From a Jewish perspective, this claim is not entirely wrong because, in Gen 17:10–14, circumcision is mandated as a sign for the people of God. But Paul argues that faith is prior to the law and the basis of justification. Abraham was called by God before the law, and he was justified through faith. While the law is summed up in a single commandment of love of neighbor (Gal 5:14), faith is what perfects the law. So Paul says in Gal 5:6, "For in Christ Jesus neither circumcision nor uncircumcision counts for anything; the only thing that counts is faith working through love."

As in Romans, Paul's gospel is consistent in Galatians. The good news is that anyone can become a child of God through faith. This faith is based on Christ's faithfulness (Gal 2:16), as we saw in Rom 3:21–26. Paul articulates his gospel in Galatians and defends it. His approach to the gospel is very logical: the letter opening (Gal 1:1–10), the origin of the gospel (Gal 1:11–24), the clarification of the gospel (Gal 2:1–21), the root of the gospel (Gal 3:1–29), the advantage of the gospel (Gal 4:1–31), the mandate of the gospel (Gal 5:1–6:10), and the letter conclusion (6:11–18).

Outline of Galatians

1:1–10 The Letter Opening[10]

    1:1–5 Greeting

    1:6–10 Confusion about the Gospel

---

10. See Kim, *Rereading Galatians*, 12. For a short commentary on Galatians, see Brigitte Kahl, "Galatians," in *New Testament: Fortress Commentary*, 503–25. For a rhetorical commentary on Galatians, see Hans D. Betz, *Galatians* (Philadelphia: Fortress, 1979). For a feminist commentary on Galatians, see Carolyn Osiek, "Galatians," in *The Women's Bible Commentary*, ed. Carol A. Newsom and Sharon Ringe (Louisville: Westminster John Knox, 1992), 333–37. For an African American reading of Galatians, Brad R. Braxton, "Galatians," in *True to Our Native Land*, 333–47. For a contextual reading of Galatians, see Néstor Oscar Miguéz, "Galatians," in the *Global Bible Commentary*, 463–72.

1:11–24 The Origin of the Gospel

    1:11–17 God's Revelation of Jesus Christ

    1:18–24 Independent of Jerusalem Churches

2:1–21 The Clarification of the Gospel

    2:1–10 The Gospel at the Council of Jerusalem

    2:11–14 The Case with Peter

    2:15–21 Justification through Christ Jesus's Faithfulness

3:1–29 The Root of the Gospel

    3:1–5 Confusion in the Church Due to the Lack of Faith

    3:6–12 The Gospel through Abraham's Faith

    3:13–16 Receiving the Promise of the Spirit through Christ

    3:17–18 The Gospel Rooted in God's Promise

    3:19–21 God's Promises Do Not Depend on the Law

    3:22–25 The Gospel through Jesus Christ's Faithfulness

    3:26–29 A New Vision of the Community in Christ

4:1–31 The Advantage of the Gospel

    4:1–7 God's Assurance of His Children

    4:8–11 How Can You Turn Back Again to the Elemental Spirits?

    4:12–20 Return to the Gospel

    4:21–31 "We Are Children, Not of the Slave but of the Free Woman"

5:1–6:10 The Mandate of the Gospel

    5:1–15 "Stand Firm in Christ; Do Not Submit Again to a Yoke of Slavery"

    5:16–26 Live the Spirit

    6:1–10 "Fulfill the Law of Christ"

6:11–18 The Letter Conclusion

Philippians

Paul wrote Philippians from prison to the believers in Philippi, a city in eastern Macedonia. The atmosphere of the letter reflects his last days in prison. Like 2 Corinthians, this, too, is a composite letter, made up of possibly three distinct correspondences: letter A (Phil 4:10–20), letter B (Phil 1:1–3:1; 4:21–23), and letter C (Phil 3:2–4:1).

Philippians is a warm letter that does not show a vast array of community issues. Paul renews his friendship with this church. He thanks them for their financial support and participation in his ministry. He advises them to "be of the same mind" with Christ (Phil 2:2). Here, he cites a hymn of Christ (Phil 2:6–11) to highlight the spirit of Christ and his humbling service to others. Paul also addresses false teachings about law and circumcision (Phil 3:2–21) and exhorts the church to be aware of all those who do evil works. He does not absolutize his Jewish identity because Christ is everything for him. He says in Phil 3:4–6, "Even though I, too, have reason for confidence in the flesh. If anyone else has reason to be confident in the flesh, I have more: circumcised on the eighth day, a member of the people of Israel, of the tribe of Benjamin, a Hebrew born of Hebrews; as to the law, a Pharisee; as to zeal, a persecutor of the church; as to righteousness under the law, blameless."

Outline of Philippians

4:10–20 Letter A (Thanking the Philippians for Their Support of Paul)[11]

1:1–3:1; 4:21–23 Letter B (Exhortations to the Philippians)

3:2–4:1 Letter C (Additional Exhortation)

11. For a short commentary on Philippians, see Julia Lambert Fogg, "Philippians," in *New Testament: Fortress Commentary*, 543–56.

1 Thessalonians

Paul wrote this letter to thank the Thessalonians for their good work in faith. This letter is the earliest in the New Testament (about 50 CE) and, like Philippians, is a warm letter. There were not any serious issues in this early small house church. Paul worked to support himself so that he did not have to burden them with his financial needs. Most of the community members were gentiles from a low economic class. Some Thessalonians worried about those who were dying prior to Christ's return. Paul emphasized the validity of the resurrection of the dead and comforted them with the promise that God would take care of them (1 Thess 4:14–17). Some did not work because they were anticipating the coming of the Lord. Paul warned that they should work until the Lord comes back. They must show good conduct among the gentiles (1 Thess 4:1–5:11). Some were persecuted or in trouble because of their new faith. Paul encouraged them to continue in that faith. Paul's main teaching is found in 1 Thess 1:9–10: "For the people of those regions report about us what kind of welcome we had among you, and how you turned to God from idols, to serve a living and true God, and to wait for his Son from heaven, whom he raised from the dead—Jesus, who rescues us from the wrath that is coming."

Outline of 1 Thessalonians

1:1 Opening[12]

1:2–2:16 Thanksgiving

2:17–3:13 Timothy's Mission

4:1–5:24 Exhortations

5:26–28 Closing

---

12. For a short commentary on 1 Thessalonians, see Edward Pillar, "1 Thessalonians," in *New Testament: Fortress Commentary*, 573–82.

Philemon

The shortest of Paul's letters, Philemon is—according to traditional interpretation—a personal correspondence between Paul and a Christian named Philemon, whose slave, Onesimus, had run away and found Paul. Paul's view of slavery is variously interpreted in this letter. He writes this letter from prison and sends it to "Philemon our dear friend and co-worker, to Apphia our sister, to Archippus our fellow soldier, and to the church in your house" (Phlm 1:1–2). Onesimus is with Paul and serves him during his imprisonment. Paul sends him back to Philemon with his letter, hoping Philemon will accept him and return Onesimus back to him. For this purpose, Paul appeals to Philemon's mercy or love. Some say that Paul is very sensitive and careful about this issue because he does not want to push Philemon to an extreme.[13] Others say that Paul is passive about this issue of slavery and does not voice his abolitionist position. Still other interpreters point out that the text does not explicitly state that Onesimus is a slave of Philemon or is a fugitive. He may be "a slave that Philemon loaned to Paul for a set time," or "Paul's apprentice," or "Philemon's estranged brother."[14] Overall, this short personal letter reveals Paul's utmost care for Onesimus and his careful communication with Philemon to achieve his goal. Though Paul is not an abolitionist as we wish him to be, his love for both Philemon and Onesimus should be noted.

Outline of Philemon

1:1–3 Greeting[15]

1:4–7 Love and Fictive Kinship Language[16]

1:8–22 Appeal

1:23–25 Benediction

13. For an interpretation history of Philemon, see Demetrius K. Williams, "'No Longer as a Slave': Reading the Interpretation History of Paul's Epistle to Philemon," in *Onesimus Our Brother: Reading Religion, Race, and Culture in Philemon*, ed. Matthew Johnson, James Noel, and Demetrius Williams (Minneapolis: Fortress, 2012), 11–45.

14. Smith and Kim, *Toward Decentering the New Testament*, 273.

15. For a short commentary on Philemon, see Eric D. Barreto, "Philemon," in *New Testament: Fortress Commentary*, 613–23.

16. Barreto, 274.

SUMMARY

Overall, in his undisputed letters, Paul claims that the good news of God was confirmed through Jesus Christ, who was faithful to God and humanity. Through Christ's faithfulness, all who come to God are justified. While a new time and a new life began with Christ, his followers have to continue to die and live with him. They must be led by the Spirit and share in Christ's faithfulness. Paul is eager to let the world know about this good news of God that came through Jesus that all people can become children of God through faith. For this gospel, Paul was called as an apostle (Rom 1:1) and engaged in tireless missionary journeys.

3

THE GOSPEL (GOOD NEWS)

OVERVIEW

Euangelion in Greek means "good news" or "gospel." In this book, *good news* and *gospel* are used interchangeably. The term does not originate with Paul. It appears frequently in the synoptic Gospels and elsewhere in the New Testament.[1] In Mark 1:14, the first thing Jesus does after baptism by John is proclaim "the good news of God." In Mark, the good news has a double entendre: the good news that Jesus proclaims (i.e., "the good news of God") and the good news about Jesus who brings good news to people. Jesus announces God's new rule or new order and asks people to turn their minds toward God. He says in Mark 1:15, "The time is fulfilled, and the kingdom of God has come near; repent, and believe in the good news."[2] Jesus's primary work has to do with the good news of God, which is about or from God. The good news does not come from Rome, and it is not about Caesar. This good news is about the new rule or reign of God, as it is expressed in "the good news of the kingdom of God" (Luke 4:43; 8:1; 16:16)

---

1. C. Clifton Black, "Good News of the New Testament," Bible Odyssey, accessed January 28, 2020, https://tinyurl.com/yydfa9cc.

2. Here in Mark 1:15, "time" is *kairos* in Greek, which indicates God's special time or the season that God rules the world. Therefore, people must repent and accept the reign of God. Here "repentance" means to change a mind and live by the reign of God.

or "the good news of the kingdom" (Matt 4:23; 9:35; 24:14). The good news is that God's new reign has come to the world in the here and now. It also envisions a new world of peace and justice, as Isaiah says: "Every valley shall be lifted up, and every mountain and hill be made low; the uneven ground shall become level, and the rough places a plain" (Isa 40:4). There is no single word for the "good news" in John's gospel. But it does not mean that John does not have the good news of God. In John, the good news of God has to do with the Logos of God that Jesus embodies in a world where there is neither light nor life. In John's theological worldview, Jesus brings good news to the world through his work, delivering the word of God, exemplifying it at all costs (John 17:6, 14). To make this good news a reality, followers of Jesus have to keep his word. Mere belief in him is not enough. As he says, "If you continue in my word, you are truly my disciples; and you will know the truth, and the truth will make you free" (John 8:31–32).

The idea of good news is also present in the Hebrew Bible and in Second Temple Judaism. For example, Isaiah proclaims the good message of hope about the restoration of Jerusalem, as quoted in Rom 10:15: "How beautiful upon the mountains are the feet of the messenger who announces peace, who brings good news, who announces salvation, who says to Zion, 'Your God reigns'" (Isa 52:7). Likewise, Isa 61:1 (which Jesus reads aloud in the synagogue in Luke 4:18) contains a clear message of the good news to the marginalized: "The spirit of the Lord God is upon me, because the Lord has anointed me; he has sent me to bring good news to the oppressed, to bind up the brokenhearted, to proclaim liberty to the captives, and release to the prisoners." In the Second Temple period (516 BCE–70 CE), the good news is about Jewish liberation from the foreign control of first Persia, then the Greek kingdoms, and then the Roman Empire.

The good news (*euangelion*) is also an important topic in Paul's letters. Paul is devoted to proclaiming God's gospel to the gentiles. He says in Rom 1:1, "Paul, a servant of Jesus Christ, called to be an apostle, set apart *for the gospel of God*" (italics mine). Paul elaborates the gospel variously, relating it to both God and Jesus. For him, the good news does not begin with Jesus but begins with God, and Paul relates it to Jesus and all who follow him.

GRECO-ROMAN AND JEWISH TEXTS AND CONTEXTS

Paul lived in the first century CE as a diasporic Jew, knowing Jewish culture and religion, hearing the good news about the emperor or the Roman Empire. In the Roman Empire, the good news is associated with the emperor's birthday, victory in war, and the propaganda of peace and security. The birth of Augustus is celebrated throughout the regions because he brought good news for the world. Augustus's reign (from 27 BCE to his death in 14 CE) is referred to as the "good news," as the Priene Inscription shows:

> Because Providence, which has arranged all aspects of our lives, lavishing attention and distinction on us, has set up the most perfect order for life by bringing forth Augustus, whom she filled with excellence for the benefit of humanity, having sent him—both for us and for those who will come after us—as a savior (*soter*) who will cause war to cease and will order all things; and because Caesar [Augustus], by his appearance, [surpassed] the hopes of those who received in past days, not only surpassing those who were benefactors before him, but even leaving any hope of surpassing him among those who are to come; and because the birthday of the god marked the beginning of good news (*euangelion* in plural) through him.[3]

Local leaders in Priene in Asia Minor praise the emperor as a god, saying that he is a savior whose birth was "the beginning of good news for the world." The imperial gospel begins with

---

3. Wilhelm Dittenberger, comp., *Orientis Graeci Inscriptiones Selectae*, Attalus, accessed September 28, 2020, 458, lines 32–42, https://tinyurl.com/y3occr8z (brackets in the original).

Augustus (meaning the "sacred one"), who is connected with the legendary hero of Rome, Aeneas. Virgil's *Aeneid*, a literary masterpiece of epic poetry, implies that Rome is destined to rule the world without end. Likewise, Horace writes about the Pax Augustana:

> When I wished to sing of fights and cities won, Apollo checked me, striking loud his lyre, and forbade my spreading tiny sails upon the Tuscan Sea. Your time, O Caesar, has restored to farms their plentiful crops and to our Jupiter the standards stripped from the proud columns of the Parthians; free of war, it has closed Quirinus's temple, has put a check on license by passing a just order, banished crime and called back home the ancient ways by which the Latin name and might of Italy grew great, and the fame and majesty of our dominion were stretched from the sun's western bed to its rising. While Caesar guards the state, not civil rage, nor violence, nor wrath that forges swords, embroiling hapless towns, shall banish peace.[4]

As seen previously, Augustus's gospel is "peace and security" that he brings to the world. Emperors are honored for their work and deified through minting coins and writing inscriptions. A coin minted during the time of Tiberius reads, "Tiberius Caesar, Augustus, son of the divine Augustus."[5] A marble copy awarded by the senate to Augustus reads, "The Senate and Roman people to Emperor Augustus, Caesar and Son of God, in his eighth consulship gave this shield, [to recognize his] works of virtue, mercy, justice, and piety, to the gods and his fatherland."[6] Augustus has various honorable titles: *divi filius* (son of the deified one), *princeps* (first man of the senate), and *pontifex maximus* (high priest). At the age of seventy-six, he inscribed the record of his accomplishments, which is

---

4. Horace, *Odes*, Perseus Digital Library, accessed September 28, 2020, 4.15, https://tinyurl.com/y5ppn2k4.

5. Neil Elliott and Mark Reasoner, eds., *Documents and Images for the Study of Paul* (Minneapolis: Fortress, 2011), 138.

6. Elliott and Reasoner, 136 (brackets in the original).

called *Res Gestae Divi Augusti* (*The Achievements of the Dei-fied Augustus*), on the walls of temples in cities throughout the empire. It is composed of thirty-five detailed accomplishments and helps us understand his pride in them.

Several decades later, Josephus, a Jewish historian in the first century CE, talks about the newly emerging emperor, Vespasian (ruling from 69 to 79 CE), who saves and secures the empire. He writes as follows: "The people, freed at length from terrors, acclaimed Vespasian emperor, and celebrated with one common festival both his establishment in power and the overthrow of Vitellius. On reaching Alexandria Vespasian was greeted by the good news (*euangelion* in the plural) from Rome and by embassies of congratulation from every quarter of the world, now his own; and that city, though second only to Rome in magnitude, proved too confined for the throng. The whole empire being now secured and the Roman state saved beyond expectation, Vespasian turned his thoughts to what remained in Judaea."[7]

While the Roman Empire argues that the good news comes from Rome or the god Jupiter, imperial good news does not benefit all people equally or justly. Everyday people, especially the marginalized, know that this good news is not really good for them. How can lower-class people believe such good news? How can slaves believe that Rome is a good society? What they need is freedom, justice, economic resources, homes to live, and peace of mind. The good news from Rome is only for a chosen few of elites and the wealthy. The imperial gospel is supported by Stoic philosophers who argue that society is one. The implication is that members of society have to accept their destiny and stay in their place without complaint.

In the Jewish world, messianic hope was prevalent, and people expected to see someone like King David, who would save them from foreign domination. From the Babylonian

---

7. Josephus, *Jewish War*, Lexundria, accessed September 28, 2020, 4.655–57, https://tinyurl.com/yyc5j9rv. Josephus has a pro-Roman tone as a captive and justifies Roman control of Jewish land.

exile in the sixth century BCE to Roman domination of Palestine in the first century CE, Jews were in constant peril and aspired to be an independent country freed from empires. Some Jews considered Cyrus the Great, the king of Persia, as the messiah because he allowed Jews to return to their homeland and rebuild their temple in Jerusalem (Isa 45:1; 2 Chr 36:22–23; Ezra 1:1–8). But by the fourth century BCE, they were under the control of Alexander the Great, who conquered much of the known world. Soon after Alexander died in 323 BCE, his empire was divided up among his generals. Palestine was under the control of the Seleucid Empire and the Ptolemaic Empire. King Antiochus IV Epiphanes invaded Jerusalem and desecrated the temple. This event caused a furor among the Jews, and the Maccabean revolt broke out in the second century BCE (see 1 and 2 Maccabees). Eventually, the Jews won and established their own government ruled by the Hasmonean dynasty. Jewish political control of Judea was good news according to the nationalists. The Hasmoneans governed Judaea for about a century before the Roman general Pompey invaded in 63 BCE.

In the first century CE, Rome ruled Judea. Four Jewish sects responded to the occupation differently. The Essenes withdrew to the desert at Qumran and established their own community. They rejected the establishment of the Jerusalem temple and its leadership. And they fervently waited for their messiahs to come through their community.[8] The Sadducees were the wealthy class that controlled the temple. For them, the status quo was good news, and they did not want things to change. They rejected the Oral Torah and the resurrection, both of which were central to the teachings of a rival group, the Pharisees. For Pharisees, the good news was rooted in the future messianic kingdom and a belief in resurrection. They were the practical reformers of Judaism and emphasized strict observance of the law. The Zealots ("the Fourth

8. See this sectarian community's work, *The War of the Sons of Light against the Sons of Darkness*, Digital Dead Sea Scrolls, accessed September 28, 2020, https://tinyurl.com/67p4s6r, also known as the *War Scroll*, which was found at Qumran.

Philosophy" according to Josephus) are much like the Maccabean revolutionaries who fought the Seleucid kingdom. For them, the good news was the liberation of the Jewish state from Roman rule.[9]

John the Baptist baptized Jesus and taught about the kingdom of God. His good news was that people have to repent and accept the new rule of God. While Jesus's proclamation of the good news is similar to that of John (both of them emphasize the rule of God coming now and in the future), Jesus's work is different from John's. Jesus not only declared the new rule of God but also exemplified it through his work. He advocated for the marginalized and brought good news to them: the poor, the captives, the blind, and the oppressed (see Luke 4:18–20; cf. Isa 61:1).

THE "GOSPEL" IN PAUL'S LETTERS

The gospel in Paul's undisputed letters is threefold: "the gospel of God," "the gospel of Christ," the gospel that Jesus's followers must proclaim. The good news of God means the good news about and from God. God is loving, righteous, steadfast, and faithful. God called Abraham out of nowhere and made a covenant with him. God promised Abraham that the whole world will be blessed in him. Abraham trusted God and walked in the faith until he died. This promise of blessing was fulfilled through Christ, and all those who have faith will become children of God. God's covenantal love extends to all.

The good news of God also means it comes from God, not from Rome or human masters. God's good news challenges all forms of so-called good news that are not concerned with love and justice in the world. God's good news is "the power of God for salvation" (Rom 1:16). Jesus proclaimed and exemplified "the good news of God" to the world. He did not spare his own life to demonstrate God's love and justice. He was crucified because of this. All that he did constituted the good news of Christ, which shows his grace, faith, and sacrifice.

9. Elliott and Reasoner, *Documents and Images*, 35–37.

We need to accept the good news, turn our minds toward God, and proclaim it at all costs. The good news of God that Jesus proclaimed is for us. We have to believe that God is the source of our life and proclaim the gospel to all. According to Paul, the gospel is more than a message or knowledge. The gospel is "the power of God for salvation to everyone who has faith" (Rom 1:16). The one who called us is God, and the one with whom we have fellowship is his Son, Jesus. In the following, we will briefly examine the "gospel" in the major letters of Paul.

Romans shows a threefold gospel that is God centered, Christ exemplified, and Christian imitated. The God-centered gospel means God is the initiator of the good news that he promised "through his prophets in the holy scriptures" (Rom 1:2). This good news is the power of God for salvation, and it points to God's righteousness (Rom 1:17; 3:21–22). This power of God is realized through faith and does not discriminate against any social determinants such as race, gender, or class (Rom 15:16, 20; 16:25). The Christ-exemplified gospel means God's good news needs Christ's work, his grace, and his faith (Rom 1:3; 3:21–26). God's love was confirmed through Christ's act of righteousness (Rom 5:12–21). Therefore, Jesus's followers have to share his faith, which means the gospel is Christian imitated. God justifies "the one who has *the faithfulness of Jesus*" (Rom 3:26; italics indicate my translation). When Paul refers to "my gospel," he means that he proclaims the gospel of God through Christ. Interpreters often do not see the importance of God's good news that is proclaimed by Jesus. Paul's gospel is not simply about justification by faith but about God's power that is effective for all who participate in Christ's faithfulness. We see this big picture of the gospel in Romans.[10]

Rom 1:1–17 is the synopsis of the gospel in Romans. Here we see why Paul is eager to share his gospel with the whole world, what his call is about, what his gospel is about, and what Jesus's followers should do. He is passionate about the gospel

---

10. Jewett, *Romans*, 136–47.

because it is "the power of God for salvation to everyone who has faith" (Rom 1:16). He wants to strengthen the faith of the Roman Christians rather than force them to accept his view, and he hopes to receive support from them when he goes to Spain for his final mission. His mission is to the gentiles who have not yet heard the good news. Paul's gospel is about salvation for everyone. This gospel is summarized in Rom. 1:16–17: "For I am not ashamed of the gospel; it is the power of God for salvation to everyone who has faith, to the Jew first and also to the Greek. For in it the righteousness of God is revealed through faith for faith; as it is written, 'The one who is righteous will live by faith.'"

As we saw in chapter 2, Romans can be outlined with "the gospel." Rom 1:18–11:36 is called "the gospel of faith that does not reject the law or Israel." Here, Paul argues that God's righteousness, which is the content of the gospel, was manifested through Christ Jesus's faithfulness and that it is effective for all who have faith (Rom 3:22). He talks about the benefits of the gospel, which is to become children of God and to live in Christ with freedom. But he makes clear that his gospel does not reject the law or Israel. He says faith cannot overthrow the law, which is the gift of God. The problem is not the law per se but people who insist that faith is not enough or those who do not accept Jesus as the Messiah. He holds the view that God's covenant with Israel is valid and hopes that God will save his people in the future. Yet he makes clear that both Jews and gentiles need faith to live as people of God.

Rom 12–16 should be understood as part of Paul's gospel because it talks about the gospel's power to transform community and society. Many people think that while Rom 1–8 is considered the heart of the gospel, Rom 12–16 is merely an ethical part. In this view, there is separation between faith and works. But this is not Paul's view. He never separates faith and works. For example, he emphasizes "faith working through love" (Gal 5:6). In 1 Cor 13, he says faith without love is nothing. He also says, "Knowledge puffs up, but love builds up" (1 Cor 8:1). For Paul, faith is not knowledge about God or Jesus; it is trust and loyalty that come with action.

In Galatians, Paul defends his gospel of faith.[11] The good news is that all can become children of God through faith, which means trusting God and following Jesus. This gospel originated in God, was proclaimed and exemplified by Jesus, and continues to be proclaimed by followers of Jesus. In the theme of gospel, we see the progressive development of Paul's letter: the origin of the gospel (Gal 1:11–2:10), the clarification of the gospel (Gal 2:11–21), the root of the gospel (Gal 3:1–29), the advantage of the gospel (Gal 4:1–31), the mandate of the gospel (Gal 5:1–6:10).

The origin of his gospel is in God's revelation of Jesus Christ (Gal 1:15–16). The gospel is also clarified in relation to Jewish law and culture. The gospel is effective for people who have faith. One can be justified through the way of Christ, which is Christ's faithfulness (Gal 2:16). While the law is not rejected, it is not the condition for the gospel. Paul's gospel is not law-free but string-free. That is, specific rules or works of the law such as circumcision or dietary laws are not required for gentile Christians because the gospel works with faith, as it did with Abraham.[12] The law is not outdated or replaced by the gospel or by Jesus. Rather, it is summed up in a single commandment: "You shall love your neighbor as yourself" (Gal 5:14). For Paul, the gospel is one and the same for both Jews and gentiles. The only difference is that Jews may keep their religious traditions while staying in Christ. In the end, what is essential for the gospel is neither circumcision nor uncircumcision but "faith working through love" (Gal 5:6). The gospel is rooted in God's promise to Abraham. It does not depend on the law. Christ fulfilled God's promises given to

---

11. Kim, *Rereading Galatians*.

12. The so-called New Perspective on Paul presents Paul as a Christian Jew who did not leave Judaism or reject the law. This view says Judaism in the first-century CE Palestine is not a legalistic religion but the religion of grace. Jews keep the law not to earn righteousness but to thank God as a covenant people. This idea is called "covenantal nomism." See E. P. Sanders, *Comparing Judaism and Christianity: Common Judaism, Paul, and the Inner and the Outer in Ancient Religion* (Minneapolis: Fortress, 2016), 51–83; see also Sanders, *Paul and Palestinian Judaism*, 419–30. See also James Dunn, *Jesus, Paul, and the Law: Studies in Mark and Galatians* (Louisville: Westminster John Knox, 1990), 183–206.

Abraham through faith, and now all people can become children of God through faith (the advantage of the gospel). After this, he talks about the mandate of the gospel that Jesus's followers must live by the law of faith, which means the law of Christ, or be led by the Spirit.

In 1 Corinthians, Paul responds to various issues raised by the Corinthians and implies a threefold gospel in 1:9: "God is faithful; by him you were called into the fellowship of his Son, Jesus Christ our Lord." Threefold gospel means the gospel involves God, Jesus, and Christians. The good news is about or from God, who is faithful and loving (1 Cor 1:4). By God's love, the Corinthians were called into fellowship with Jesus, who obeyed God's will and revealed God's love through his faithfulness and his sacrifice. Here, Jesus is the good news because of his grace and his faithfulness. Through his spirit, people may experience new life, and they may stand in good relationship with God. This is the good news that followers of Jesus must proclaim. Paul decided to proclaim only Christ crucified (1 Cor 2:2). Proclaiming "Christ crucified" means the Corinthians must challenge the wisdom of the world and live faithfully, being united to Christ (1 Cor 1:18–25; 6:12–20).

SUMMARY

The good news is more than salvific knowledge. It carries the power of God to everyone who has faith. The good news is also countercultural in the sense that all other news may be relativized by God's good news. Good news involves the work of Jesus and the Christian response to it. We hear various forms of good news from here and there. But the question is, What is the gospel?

The gospel derives from the Greek term *euangelion*, which means "good news." In the first century, the Roman Empire announced to the world its version of good news. The emperor Augustus was proclaimed to be divine, and he was called son of god. He boasted about his achievements and claimed that he had brought peace and security to his empire. But this good news had little significance for ordinary people. The emperor's gospel was only for a chosen few: royal families, senators, and governors. There was no salvation for the marginalized, immigrants, and foreigners. Rulers talk about peace, security, and unity in order to maintain their power. In Roman society, there were clear divisions between the haves and have-nots, educated and uneducated, Greeks and barbarians, and male and female. What about America and elsewhere in the world? What kind of gospel do we proclaim today?

Paul helps us discern what the gospel is. First, the gospel is good news about God. God is righteous, faithful, and steadfast. God cares for the poor, orphans, widows, immigrants, and sojourners. God is good news, not Rome or the emperor. It does not come from human beings. It has been promised and testified through God's prophets in the Old Testament. Paul says that he was called an apostle and set apart for the gospel of God, and the gospel of God is the key to understanding Paul's gospel.

Second, the gospel is concerned with Jesus. He faithfully demonstrated God's love in the world. Because of that, he was crucified. But God raised him from the dead. Through Jesus's work and his proclamation of the gospel of God, God's righteousness has been manifested. God's righteousness means God is the one who is righteous. God is the sun and light. Jesus revealed God through his life and death. He exemplified the love of God through his faithfulness. Rom 3:22 confirms this point: "God's righteousness is revealed through Jesus Christ's faith [*pistis christou*]" (my translation). Jesus is like the moon that reflects the sun. He is the light only because he does the work of the light.

Third, the gospel also involves followers of Jesus who share the good news with all. Paul writes Romans to share the gospel of God concerning his Son to the gentiles. In the letter, he expresses his desire to visit Rome, and ultimately, his goal is to go on a Spanish mission with the support of the Roman Christians. He says that he is "not ashamed of the gospel." This implies that there are some people who are ashamed of the gospel. From the perspective of the empire or the elites, the gospel of God is weak, foolish, and shameful because it does not promote power, status, and wealth to them. But Paul says he is not ashamed of the gospel because "it is the power of God for salvation to everyone who has faith, to the Jew first and also the Greek."

The gospel is more than knowledge about God or Jesus. It is the power of God for salvation. Note here that the gospel is the power of God. This means God empowers the downtrodden to live a new life now. Whenever and wherever the gospel is proclaimed, there must be a new life and a new community in Christ. God calls the weak and foolish into community. Paul says, "God chose what is foolish in the world to shame the wise; God chose what is weak in the world to shame the strong; God chose what is low and despised in the world, things that are not, to reduce to nothing things that are" (1 Cor 1:27–28). The power of God is not limited to Jews or Romans. It is for "everyone who has faith." It breaks down the Roman ideology of separation between Greeks and barbarians, between the educated and uneducated, and between the wise and the foolish. All are potential children of God. But the power of God needs faith. Paul writes the centerpiece of the gospel in Rom 1:17 NKJ: "For in it [the gospel] the righteousness of God is revealed from faith to faith; as it is written, 'The just shall live by faith.'" The phrase "from faith to faith" (ek pisteos eis pistin) is a difficult one to interpret. Some suggest that it is "from God's faithfulness to Jesus's faithfulness." Others say that it is "from Jesus's faithfulness to Christians' faithfulness." Still others say that it is "from one person's faith to another's." I would suggest that the previous phrase means "from Christ's faith to Christians' faith," as implied in Rom 3:22: "God's righteousness through the faith of Jesus Christ for all who have faith."

As we see earlier, the gospel has a threefold structure: the gospel of God, the gospel of Christ, and the gospel Christians need to proclaim. In all of this, the common denominator is faith. God is faithful, Jesus is faithful, and therefore, Christians should be faithful. We get a snapshot of this gospel in Rom 3:21–22: "But now, apart from law, the righteousness of God has been disclosed, and is attested by the law and the prophets, God's righteousness through the faith of Jesus Christ for all who have faith."

But what if people do not accept the gospel? The answer is found in Rom 1:18: "For the wrath of God is revealed from heaven against all ungodliness and wickedness of those who by their wickedness suppress the truth." Here "the wrath of God" is caused by those who are unfaithful. They are those who suppress the truth of God. The wrath of God is revealed now. Paul uses the present passive indicative form of the verb *apokalupto* (to reveal). The wrath of God is revealed now because they do not live by faith. It is not God's vengeance or retribution. Therefore, it is not the same as "the day of wrath" in Rom 2:5, when "God's righteous judgment will be revealed." In Rom 1:18, Paul's point is simple. If people do not participate in the power of God, they will live according to degrading passions. But the gospel does not end with the wrath of God. There is still hope for them because God is still loving. In this sense, the Christian gospel is not judgmental. The gospel is "the power of God for salvation to everyone who has faith" (Rom 1:16).

QUESTIONS FOR REFLECTION

1. What is "gospel" or "good news" according to Paul?

2. People often think the gospel usually begins with Christ ("the gospel of Christ"). Is this good enough for the gospel? How will you relate to the gospel of God and the gospel we individually proclaim in our context?

3. What kind of gospel do we need to preach in our context where many different people need different kinds of good news?

4. Is Paul's gospel law-free or string-free?

4

RIGHTEOUSNESS/ JUSTIFICATION

OVERVIEW

Tzedakah is a very important theme in the Hebrew Bible. It is usually translated as "righteousness."[1] It is the core attribute of God, who calls Abraham, protects and disciplines his people, gives hopes to the exiles, ensures justice in the world, and judges evil. God wants his people to be holy and live faithfully (Hab 2:4). For example, Lev 19:2 reads, "Speak to all the congregation of the people of Israel and say to them: You shall be holy, for I the Lord your God am holy." *Tzedakah* denotes relationship. As God is righteous, good, and just, so too should his people be, in relation both to one another and to God. Righteousness is a broad concept, encompassing all that is just or righteous.

There is a similar connotation in the word *mishpat*, which is usually translated as "justice."[2] This word refers to the need for balance, equilibrium, equity, or fairness. *Mishpat* denotes

1. For a discussion of "righteousness" in the Old Testament, see John Scullion, "Righteousness (OT)," in *Anchor Bible Dictionary*, ed. David Noel Freedman (New York: Doubleday, 1992), 5:724–36.

2. Temba Mafico, "Just, Justice," in *Anchor Bible Dictionary*, ed. David Noel Freedman (New York: Doubleday, 1992), 3:1127–29.

"fairness" in human lives, especially in matters of social justice. The term also connotes judgment or a legal claim. The prophet Amos implicitly distinguishes between righteousness and justice when he talks about injustices in society: "But let justice roll down like waters, and righteousness like an ever-flowing stream" (Amos 5:24). Amos uses his poetic imagination to challenge Israelites to live with justice *and* righteousness. Justice must run like waters and righteousness like an ever-flowing stream. Justice must be heard louder. The prophet says that God does not want festivals, burnt offerings, or noisy music. God wants to hear a loud sound of justice rolling like a river. Justice must be heard everywhere, and it requires a fair distribution of wealth and economic justice. The "waters" symbolize the vibrant, dynamic power of justice that is effective for all. The prophet then gives us the image of the "stream" and relates it to righteousness. A stream lies in the lowest valley and flows steadily and quietly. The source of a stream is rain. The image of righteousness "flowing like an ever-flowing stream" means that we depend on God for our living. We should be humble before God and others, acknowledging God's grace in our lives. In the end, we need both waters and streams in our lives. We need big waters of justice in society. Yet a big river is not made on its own. It is the confluence of many streams. But even a stream is not possible without rain. Thus justice without righteousness would be noisy music.

In the New Testament, the Greek noun *dikaiosyne* is used to convey the meaning of righteousness or justice. The proper translation or meaning of *dikaiosyne* must be determined by context. The adjective of this word is *dikaios*, and the verbal form is *dikaioo*: to put into a right relationship (with God). This verbal form complicates our translation and interpretation because we should wonder what makes us in right relationship with God.

In the New Testament, Jesus and Paul use *dik-* stem words frequently. In Matthew's gospel, Jesus says, "But strive first for the kingdom of God and his righteousness, and all these things will be given to you as well" (Matt 6:33). Jesus's point is that if people seek the way of God, the result will be a more just society in which people share what they have with one another. He also connects righteousness to baptism. When John is reluctant to baptize him, Jesus says that it is necessary in order to fulfill righteousness (Matt 3:13–17). Righteousness also appears in beatitudes: "Blessed are those who hunger and thirst for righteousness, for they will be filled" (Matt 5:6); "Blessed are those who are persecuted for righteousness' sake, for theirs is the kingdom of heaven" (Matt 5:10). Righteousness is a moral criterion for entering the kingdom of God: "For I tell you, unless your righteousness exceeds that of the scribes and Pharisees, you will never enter the kingdom of heaven" (Matt 5:20). Paul also talks about *dikaiosyne*. In Romans alone, he uses it more than thirty times, applying it to God: "the righteousness of God" (Rom 1:17; 3:21–22, 25), relating it to the human relationship with God: "Abraham believed God, and it was reckoned to him as righteousness" (Rom 4:3; quoting Gen 15:6).

GRECO-ROMAN AND JEWISH TEXTS AND CONTEXTS

There is a range of views on "justice" among ancient philosophers. Plato believes that the city should be ruled by wise people—the philosopher kings. He also believes that the soul has three parts—rational, appetitive, and spirited—and that these three parts correspond to three social ranks in society. The rational part that rules the soul corresponds to the ruling class, the appetitive part corresponds to the working class, and the spirited part corresponds to the guardian class. Justice, for Plato, results from each class fulfilling its role in society without interfering with one another.

Paul rejects this view of justice. As he says in 1 Cor 1:27, "But God chose what is foolish in the world to shame the wise; God chose what is weak in the world to shame the strong." In Plato's logic, this act of God is foolish. But this act is justice for Paul.

Aristotle's view of justice is different from Plato's. As he says in his *Nicomachean Ethics*, "In this sense justice is complete virtue. It is often regarded as the highest virtue, because its end is virtue in its complete sense in that the individual exercises it in relation to another person and not just himself."[3] Aristotle considers justice as a virtue that needs to be developed. He also recognizes two different forms of justice: the universal and the particular. As he continues in the same book, "Universal justice is concerned with obeying laws and with virtue as a whole. Particular justice is seen as one of the virtues and is divided into two kinds: distributive and corrective. Distributive justice involves distributing honors, money and other assets. Corrective justice has two parts: voluntary transactions involving paying debts, buying and selling, and so on; and involuntary transactions involving the giving of just restitution of harms inflicted."[4] Aristotle is concerned with the ethical and practical side of justice and its benefits for everyday people. When persons act together in a manner informed by practical wisdom, the result is a just community. And when a community is just, it helps form persons to act justly. Practical wisdom is cultivated through learning from and imitating those who are morally excellent and wise. Aristotle's practical sense of wisdom is compatible with Paul's view that ethical conduct must be cultivated and modeled after Christ.

Stoics in the Roman Empire, though varied, consider justice an important virtue. For example, the Roman Stoic philosopher Cicero (106–43 BCE) affirms Plato's four cardinal virtues. As he says, "Virtue may be defined as a habit of mind (*animi*) in harmony with reason and the order of nature. It has four parts: wisdom, justice, courage, temperance."[5] Cicero considers justice to be "the principle which constitutes the bond of human society and of a virtual community of life."[6] As a Stoic,

3. Aristotle, *Nicomachean Ethics*, Internet Classics Archive, accessed September 28, 2020, 5.2.1130a14–b29, https://tinyurl.com/pujm5kw.

4. Aristotle, *Nicomachean Ethics*, 5.2.1130b30–1131a1; 5.4.1132a18.

5. Cicero, *De Inventione*, University of Waterloo, accessed September 28, 2020, II, LIII, https://tinyurl.com/y5dszo79. Four Macc 1:18: "Now the kinds of wisdom are rational judgment, justice, courage, and self-control."

6. Cicero, *De Officiis*, Bill Thayer (website), accessed September 28, 2020, https://tinyurl.com/yx8vr9l8.

he emphasizes the importance of self-control and the common good of society. This kind of philosophy helps everyday people struggling to live in a harsh environment find courage and peace of mind. But it does not advocate for or liberate the weak and marginalized. Stoicism discourages protest against the status quo and allows inequalities and injustices to continue to determine people's lives, as we see in the fable of Menenius.[7] Stoics were elites. They did not care about the destiny of the marginalized; rather, they supported the ideology of hierarchical unity in society.

We see both similarities and differences between the concepts of justice that Greco-Roman philosophers advocated and the view advanced by Paul. Paul, as a Hellenistic Jew, was familiar with Stoic philosophy, and he accepted the idea of unity or oneness at least to some extent, as he writes in 1 Cor 12 and Rom 12. But unlike the Stoics, his view of community is egalitarian, and his notion of justice is based on God's justice, not human justice. For Paul, humans are to follow God's justice and cultivate virtue by imitating Christ's example.

To understand Pauline and other Hellenistic Jewish ideas of justice, we need to view Jewish texts and history in the context of the Maccabean revolt in the second century BCE (1 Macc 1:41–49) and the rule of the Roman Empire in the first century CE. Given God's promises to the people of Israel, his justice was called into question when innocent people suffered and died from the second century BCE to the first century CE under a succession of invading foreign forces.

The prophet Daniel argues that God rewards the innocent martyrs and will restore Israel in the future (Dan 12:1–3). First Maccabees describes the heroic deaths of the Maccabean brothers who fought for God's justice, while 2 Maccabees emphasizes the importance of martyrdom and piety for God that result in the reward of resurrection and the afterlife. While 1 Maccabees aims at legitimating the Hasmonean dynasty, 2 Maccabees deals more with God's justice in ways

7. Livy, *History of Rome*, Perseus Digital Library, accessed September 28, 2020, 2.32.9–12, https://tinyurl.com/y4kd62n4.

that show God protecting his people when they are loyal to the covenant and punishing their enemies (2 Macc 2:19–23).

In the first century CE in Palestine, different sects within Judaism variously responded to the situation under the Roman Empire. While the Zealots fought for God's justice against the Romans, the Pharisees were interested in the renewal of the law. The Sadducees benefitted from Roman rule, while the Essenes gave scathing criticisms of the established leadership in the temple and had their own vision of righteousness in their community at Qumran (CD 1:1, 11, 15–16; 20:32).

RIGHTEOUSNESS/JUSTIFICATION IN PAUL'S LETTERS

Dikaiosyne-related words appear more than thirty times in Romans, as well as in Galatians and both 1 and 2 Corinthians. The phrase "the righteousness of God" appears frequently in Romans.[8] In Rom 1:17, Paul says that in the gospel, the righteousness of God is revealed from faith to faith. The content of the gospel is "God's righteousness," which is the central theme of Romans. "The righteousness of God" means that God is righteous, is faithful, is loving, protects the poor and weak, and judges evil.[9] People depend on his righteousness by living faithfully. God called Abraham and promised that the world will be blessed in him. Abraham trusted God, but God's promise was not fulfilled until Christ came. "But now," says Paul, "apart from law, the righteousness of God has been disclosed, and is attested by the law and the prophets, the righteousness of God through faith in Jesus Christ for all who believe" (Rom 3:21–22). Here "but now" is an emphatic point about Christ, that he became a new seed of hope. As Paul explains, "If, because of the one man's trespass, death exercised dominion

8. "The righteousness of God" frequently appears in Romans 1:17; 3:5, 21, 22, 25–26; 10:3.

9. Katherine Grieb, The Story of Romans: A Narrative Defense of God's Righteousness (Louisville: Westminster John Knox, 2002), 19–41. See also Michael Bird, The Saving Righteousness of God: Studies on Paul, Justification and the New Perspective (Eugene, OR: Wipf and Stock, 2007), 6–39.

through that one, much more surely will those who receive the abundance of grace and the free gift of righteousness exercise dominion in life through the one man, Jesus Christ. Therefore just as one man's trespass led to condemnation for all, so one man's act of righteousness leads to justification and life for all" (Rom 5:17–18). Paul's point is that with Christ's faithfulness, God's righteousness has been manifested. While we will see more about Christ's faithfulness in the next chapter, notice here Christ's faithfulness is the means of revealing God's righteousness.

"God's righteousness coming through Christ's faithfulness" is effective "to all who have faith." God's saving power cannot be a reality unless we respond to it through Jesus Christ. So "to all who have faith" means Christian participation in Christ's work of God. Faith is not only to accept Jesus's salvific death but also to follow his spirit and his faithfulness. Those who participate in Christ's life and death can experience the love of God and must in turn show God's righteousness to the world. In 2 Cor 5:21, Paul also asserts the importance of Christian participation in God's righteousness: "For our sake he [Jesus] made him to be sin who knew no sin, so that in him we might become the righteousness of God." Jesus lost his life because he did the dangerous job of demonstrating God's righteousness in the world. His followers must continue to show the righteousness of God by doing the work of justice in society. When they do so, they are called children of God and justified by God. Rom 3:26 also states this idea: "It was to prove at the present time that he himself is righteous and that he justifies the one who has *the faithfulness of Jesus*" (italics indicate my translation). One's justification comes through faith, as in Rom 4:13: "For the promise that he would inherit the world did not come to Abraham or to his descendants through the law but through the righteousness of faith." "The righteousness of faith" means that righteousness comes through faith (see also Rom 9:30; 10:6).

The law is not the condition for justification. In Rom 9–11, Paul says the problem is not the law but rather the refusal to submit to God's righteousness. Rom 10:3–4 reads, "For, being ignorant of the righteousness that comes from God, and seeking to establish their own, they have not submitted to God's righteousness. For Christ is the end of the law so that there may be righteousness for everyone who believes." The problem is twofold: (1) Israel did not accept Jesus as the Messiah who fulfilled the law through his life, and (2) it did not seek God's righteousness that comes through faith. Paul's articulation of the gospel does not reject Israel or the law. He says that the law is good and holy (Rom 7:12) and that it provides guidelines for life, but it should not replace faith. It should work with faith. It is not an absolute condition for justification. Faith must inform the law, and the law must be centered on the love of neighbor (Rom 13:8–10).

Similarly, in Galatians, Paul argues that a right relationship with God is possible through Christ's faithfulness. As he says in Gal. 2:16–17, "Yet we know that a person is justified not by the works of the law but through *Jesus Christ's faithfulness*. And we have come to believe in Christ Jesus, so that we might be justified by *Christ's faithfulness*, and not by doing the works of the law, because no one will be justified by the works of the law. But if, in our effort to be justified in Christ, we ourselves have been found to be sinners, is Christ then a servant of sin? Certainly not!" (italics indicate my translation). Here as before, one's justification depends on Christ's faithfulness. *Pistis christou* in Gal 2:16–17 may be translated as "faith in Christ," which is acceptable as long as we emphasize Christian participation in Christ. But the question is whose faith Paul talks about here. Is it a believer's faith in Christ or Christ's faithfulness through which a believer must live? In my interpretation, *pistis christou* must be "Christ's faithfulness," which is the basis of Christian faith. This way, we may understand better Paul's emphasis on Christ's love, grace, and sacrifice. And all of these may be understood as aspects of Christ's faithfulness.

While "the works of the law" such as circumcision or dietary laws are not wrong in themselves, they should not be imposed on the gentiles. What matters is neither circumcision nor uncircumcision but "faith working through love" (Gal 5:6). Similarly, Rom 2:29 reads, "Rather, a person is a Jew who is one inwardly, and real circumcision is a matter of the heart—it is spiritual and not literal. Such a person receives praise not from others but from God." The whole point of faith is also seen in Gal 3:11: "Now it is evident that no one is justified before God by the law; for 'the one who is righteous will live by faith'" (cf. Rom 1:17). Paul finds the root of justification language in Abraham: "Just as Abraham 'believed God, and it was reckoned to him as righteousness,' so, you see, those who believe are the descendants of Abraham" (Gal 3:6–7).

God's promises made to Abraham were fulfilled through Jesus and his faithfulness. As Paul writes in Gal 3:13–16,

> Christ redeemed us from the curse of the law by becoming a curse for us—for it is written, "Cursed is everyone who hangs on a tree"—in order that in Christ Jesus the blessing of Abraham might come to the gentiles, so that we might receive the promise of the Spirit through faith. Brothers and sisters, I give an example from daily life: once a person's will has been ratified, no one adds to it or annuls it. Now the promises were made to Abraham and to his offspring; it does not say, "And to offsprings," as of many; but it says, "And to your offspring," that is, to one person, who is Christ.

Paul's point is that the promise God made to Abraham is finally fulfilled through Jesus, who "redeemed us from the curse of the law by becoming a curse for us." Here "Christ's redemption of us from the curse of the law" can be understood in the context of churches in Galatia where some Jewish Christians were attaching strings to Paul's gospel.[10] These strings included mandatory circumcision as well as other Jewish customs and interpretations of the law. Paul argues that if one is under the law or lives by it, there is no freedom,

---

10. Kim, *Rereading Galatians*, 61–64.

since there is no faith at its foundation. That is the curse of the law. His point is not that the law is an impossible means of salvation but that one must live by faith, as Christ "gave himself for our sins to set us free from the present evil age, according to the will of our God and Father" (Gal 1:4). Christ overcame the law's control or absolutism and fulfilled the law of God by faith. That is where Gal 5:4 warns the Galatians, "You who want to be justified by the law have cut yourselves off from Christ; you have fallen away from grace." Similarly, Gal 2:21 reads, "I do not nullify the grace of God; for if righteousness comes through the law, then Christ died for nothing." In Philippians, Paul has a similar view of righteousness "that comes through Jesus Christ for the glory and praise of God" (Phil 1:11). Likewise, in Phil 3:9, he talks about righteousness "that comes through *Christ's faithfulness*, the righteousness from God based on faith" (italics indicate my translation).

SUMMARY

In this chapter, we have explored God's righteousness as it is manifested through Christ's faithfulness. God's righteousness may be understood as God's covenantal love, saving power, and justice that defies both Roman and other traditions of merely human justice. God is righteous because he is merciful and loving to all. God is also just and concerned about injustice in the world. We need to elaborate on God's righteousness in the context of Paul's theology. God is the one who is righteous. He is like the sun that shines on all people. God is impartial and merciful to all. God is our hope and source of life. God is the foundation of everlasting hope. All of this was exemplified through Christ and his work. That is why Paul can claim that nothing can separate us from the love of God in Christ (Rom 8:38–39). In the love of God and Christ, Christians can feel secure and live confidently.

For Paul, God's righteousness also involves his saving power. We are saved from darkness and become servants of righteousness when we follow Jesus and the Spirit. In Rom 8:13,

Paul is specific about what it means to follow Jesus. It means to be led by the Spirit. To live the righteousness of God is to live according to the words of the prophet Micah: "to do justice, and to love kindness, and to walk humbly with your God" (Mic 6:8).

The other emphasis of this chapter is Paul's theology of justification. The question is, What makes us justified before God? A common interpretation of Paul insists that Jesus did everything necessary for justification and that the only thing required to receive the benefit of justification is to believe it. But as we have seen, Paul teaches that we have to *participate* in Christ's faithfulness, not merely believe that Christ is faithful. As he argues in Gal 2:16, "We are set right with God not by the works of the law, but through Christ's faithfulness." Or again in Rom 3:26, Paul writes, "God would justify the one who has the faithfulness of Jesus" (my translation). In Gal 2:20, Paul decides to live by Christ's faithfulness. For Paul, Hab 2:4 offers an important clarification for understanding faithfulness and participation: The righteous one will live by faith. Faith is fidelity or loyalty to God that makes one justified before God. As Abraham believed God, he was considered righteous. Justification needs genuine faith, and such faith is exemplified in Christ's own faithfulness. Christ made God's promises made to Abraham and his descendants a reality for all. By understanding Paul's teaching on justification and faithfulness in this way, we can better understand his warning that cheap grace is not an option (see Rom 6:1–23). When Paul asks, "Should we continue in sin in order that grace may abound?" the answer is no, because Christians are Christians inasmuch as they imitate Jesus and his faithfulness.

QUESTIONS FOR REFLECTION

1. How can you translate "the righteousness of God" in Rom 1:17 and 3:21–22? In what sense is God righteous? What does God's righteousness have to do with Christ and us?

2. Does "the righteousness of God" include the concept of justice? What can we say about its implication to matters of social justice?

3. What is justification by God? How does it happen?

4. What is the relationship between justification and sanctification?

5. How can we avoid the trap of "cheap grace"?

5

FAITHFULNESS

OVERVIEW

God's righteousness or covenantal faithfulness to Abraham does not change.[1] His impartial love for all people does not change. That is what faithfulness means. Deut 7:9 reads, "Know therefore that the Lord your God is God, the faithful God who maintains covenant loyalty with those who love him and keep his commandments, to a thousand generations" (see also Deut 32:4). The Hebrew verbal root form of "faithful" is *aman*, which has to do with confirming, supporting, nourishing, or trusting. God's faithfulness means God is trustworthy because he confirms his covenant or love. The noun form of this verb is *emunah*, which means steadfastness, faithfulness, and trust. God is steadfastness. For example, Gen 24:27 reads, "Blessed be the Lord, the God of my master Abraham, who has not forsaken his steadfast love and his faithfulness toward my master." Ps 57:10 also reads, "For your steadfast love is as high as the heavens; your faithfulness extends to the clouds" (see also Exod 34:6; Jer 31:3). *Emunah* also applies to humans. As God is faithful toward his people, they also must show faithfulness to God. For example, Josh 24:14 reads, "Now therefore revere the Lord, and serve him in sincerity and in faithfulness; put away the gods that your ancestors served beyond

1. James Price, "God's Righteousness Shall Prevail," *Interpretation* 28, no. 3 (1974): 259–80.

the River and in Egypt, and serve the Lord." Ps 26:3 also reads, "For your steadfast love is before my eyes, and I walk in faithfulness to you" (see also 1 Sam 26:23; 1 Kgs 2:4).

In the New Testament, Jesus talks about the love and faithfulness of God. In Matt 6:30, he says, "But if God so clothes the grass of the field, which is alive today and tomorrow is thrown into the oven, will he not much more clothe you—you of little faith?" (cf. Luke 12:28). Jesus's point is that God is faithful toward his creation and people. The Matthean Jesus also talks about God's impartial love in Matt 5:43–48:

> You have heard that it was said, "You shall love your neighbor and hate your enemy." But I say to you, Love your enemies and pray for those who persecute you, so that you may be children of your Father in heaven; for he makes his sun rise on the evil and on the good, and sends rain on the righteous and on the unrighteous. For if you love those who love you, what reward do you have? Do not even the tax collectors do the same? And if you greet only your brothers and sisters, what more are you doing than others? Do not even the gentiles do the same? Be perfect, therefore, as your heavenly Father is perfect.

Because God is loving and faithful, so too must his people live lovingly and faithfully. The Markan Jesus tells his disciples to have "faith in God" (Mark 11:22–25) because God hears them faithfully. He says they could do anything if they do not doubt in their heart and ask for it in prayer. The Johannine Jesus comforts his disciples by asking them to have faith in him and also in God. Jesus is faithful to God and his mission. He never abandons on his mission to teach and embody God's reign in the world.

Paul also talks about "faithfulness" in his letters. In Greek, *pistis* (or *fides* in Latin) means faithfulness, fidelity, loyalty, or trustworthiness.[2] God is righteous (Rom 1:17; 3:21–22) and faithful (1 Cor 1:9; 10:13; 2 Cor 1:18). God's faithfulness means

---

2. Daniel Smith, *Into the World of the New Testament: Greco-Roman and Jewish Texts and Contexts* (New York: T&T Clark, 2015), 172.

God keeps his covenant with humanity even when his people do not. For Paul, it is because God is faithful that he sent his Son to deal with the sins and the unfaithfulness of humanity (1 Cor 1:9; Rom 8:1–4). Paul also ascribes faithfulness to Jesus and argues that by being faithful to God, Jesus demonstrates his righteousness. Lastly, faithfulness also applies to the followers of Jesus, who must imitate Jesus's faithfulness in order to be his followers. As God is faithful to his covenantal love, so also must humans show their faithfulness through Christ.

GRECO-ROMAN AND JEWISH TEXTS AND CONTEXTS

According to Roman propaganda, the emperor is loyal to the gods and responsible for providing peace and security to the world. The emperor's subjects, by implication, imitate him and show him loyalty as an expression of their fidelity to the gods.[3] If they do not, they challenge the divine will. The Roman emperor Augustus is considered the embodiment of divine virtues and "a divine guarantor of good things to the world."[4] Because he was chosen by the gods to fulfill their will in the world, he received from them divine virtues such as *victoria* (military power to defeat enemies), *pax* (peace), *concord* (social harmony), *clementia* (mercy), *fides* (faith or loyalty), *iustitia* (justice), and *spes* (hope). These virtues are frequently seen in literature, on coins, and in art throughout the Roman world. On the Priene Inscription, Augustus's virtues are detailed. On the coin dedicated to the emperor Caesar, these words are found: "To the Mercy of Caesar." Augustus's thirty-five virtuous achievements are written on the *Res Gestae Divi Augusti*. Along with these virtues, Augustus emphasizes his piety (*pietas*) with the phrase "for the gods of Rome, his ancestors, and his household."[5] Neil Elliott explains the image of Augustus in

---

3. The Greek word *pistis* and the Latin word *fides* mean primarily the concept of "faithfulness," "loyalty," or "fidelity." For more, see Smith, *World of the New Testament*, 172–74.

4. Elliott and Reasoner, *Documents and Images*, 125.

5. Elliott and Reasoner, 131.

the Museo Palazzo Massimo in Rome: "His toga is pulled over his head in the gesture of worship; he extends his hands to offer sacrifice. Both his revitalization of Roman temples and his legislation concerning marriage were intended as reforms expressing his concern for traditional Roman values."[6] Augustus's title of Pontifex Maximus fits well with this image of him.

Faithfulness was not a concern only of the political and religious elites of Rome. Jewish thinkers of the same period gave considerable attention to the concept. The most influential Hellenistic Jewish philosopher of the first century, Philo of Alexandria, wrote, "Faith [*pistis*] in God, then, is the one sure and infallible good."[7] Philo praises Abraham's faith for his trust in God, not by words alone, but by action.[8] Because Abraham trusts in God, God rewards him. Without emphasizing the covenantal love for Jews, he universalizes the moral teachings of Torah that humans must have faith in God, not in the world, possessions, or fame. He defends Judaism and Torah by emphasizing the superiority of its moral teachings. And yet Philo does not develop countercultural or anti-imperial teachings from the liberation narratives of Exodus.

The Maccabean revolutionaries and the various Jewish sects of the first century CE also had distinct ideas about faith. Second Maccabees 2:19–23 commends martyrs because they are faithful to Judaism:

> The story of Judas Maccabeus and his brothers, and the purification of the great temple, and the dedication of the altar, and further the wars against Antiochus Epiphanes and his son Eupator, and the appearances that came from heaven to those *who fought bravely for Judaism*, so that though few in number they seized the whole land and pursued the barbarian hordes, and regained possession of the temple famous throughout the world, and liberated the city, and re-established the laws that

6. Elliott and Reasoner, 131.

7. Philo, *On Abraham*, Early Christian Writings, accessed September 28, 2020, 268, https://tinyurl.com/y5jnkjwz.

8. Philo, 262–63.

were about to be abolished, while the Lord with great kindness became gracious to them—all this, which has been set forth by Jason of Cyrene in five volumes, we shall attempt to condense into a single book. (italics mine)

The use of *Ioudaismos* (Judaism) in 2 Macc 2:21 is the first in Jewish literature. It means the Jewish way of life and religion. The martyrs of the Jewish cause will be raised from the dead because of their faith: "You accursed wretch, you dismiss us from this present life, but the King of the universe will raise us up to an everlasting renewal of life, because we have died for his laws" (2 Macc 7:9). Dan 12:2 also confirms the resurrection of the innocent martyrs to everlasting life.

In the first century CE, four distinct Jewish sects had four distinct conceptions of faith and its demands. The Zealots enacted their faith through armed rebellion against Rome. The dominant groups, the Pharisees and the Sadducees, also had contrasting ideas about faith. As Josephus writes,

But then as to the two other orders at first mentioned, the Pharisees are those who are esteemed most skillful in the exact explication of their laws, and introduce the first sect. These ascribe all to fate [or providence], and to God, and yet allow, that to act what is right, or the contrary, is principally in the power of men; although fate does co-operate in every action. They say that all souls are incorruptible, but that the souls of good men only are removed into other bodies, but that the souls of bad men are subject to eternal punishment. But the Sadducees are those that compose the second order, and take away fate entirely, and suppose that God is not concerned in our doing or not doing what is evil; and they say, that to act what is good, or what is evil, is at men's own choice, and that the one or the other belongs so to every one, that they may act as they please. They also take away the belief of the immortal duration of the soul, and the punishments and rewards in Hades. Moreover, the Pharisees are friendly to one another, and are for the exercise of concord, and regard for the public; but the behaviour of the Sadducees one towards another is in some degree wild, and their conversation with those that are of their own party is as barbarous as if they were strangers to them. And this is what I had to say concerning the philosophic sects among the Jews.[9]

The Pharisees are moderate in their response to national tragedy. They focus on reforming the law and daily lives of the Jewish people. They believe in God's providence, the resurrection, and eternal punishment. For the Pharisees, faith is about strictly keeping the law. By contrast, the Sadducees do not believe God's providence or his involvement in the world. They do not believe in the immortality of the soul. They are wealthy people who maintain their power and privilege through their control of the temple.

The fourth and most mysterious sect, the Essenes, had a still different notion of faith. As Josephus describes them,

For there are three philosophical sects among the Jews. The followers of the first of which are the Pharisees, of the second, the Sadducees, and the third sect, which pretends to a severer discipline, are called Essenes. These last are Jews by birth, and seem to have a greater affection for one another than the other sects have. These Essenes reject pleasures as an evil, but esteem continence, and the conquest over our passions to be virtue. They neglect wedlock, but choose out other persons children while they are pliable, and fit for learning, and esteem them to be of their kindred, and form them according to their own manners. They do not absolutely deny the fitness of marriage, and the succession of mankind thereby continued; but they guard against the lascivious behaviour of women, and are persuaded that none of them preserve their fidelity to one man.[10]

The Essenes favor asceticism and live in a desert community. Their faith is sectarian, and they reject the established leadership in Jerusalem and the temple. They believe that they alone are truthful and faithful toward God.

9. Josephus, *Jewish War*, 2.8.14 (brackets in the original).
10. Josephus, 2.8.2.

FAITHFULNESS IN PAUL'S LETTERS

In his letters, Paul deals often with the theme of faith and talks about God's faithfulness, Christ's faithfulness, and Christians' faithfulness.

Romans

In Romans, Paul argues that God is faithful because he has covenantal love for all, which may be understood as his righteousness. God's covenantal love for all is important, as Paul says in Rom 1:16: "For I am not ashamed of the gospel; it is the power of God for salvation *to everyone who has faith, to the Jew first and also to the Greek*" (italics mine). Even though his primary mission is to the gentiles, he acknowledges the power of the gospel for all, Jews and gentiles. God's righteousness was manifested through Christ's faithfulness (Rom 3:21–22). God will justify the one who has the faithfulness of Jesus (Rom 3:26). This threefold nature of faithfulness is also seen in Rom 1:17: "For in it *God's righteousness is revealed from faith to faith*; as it is written, 'The one who is righteous will live by faith'" (italics indicate my translation). "From faith to faith" (*ek pisteos eis pistin*) may mean interpersonal faith, as the NIV translates: "by faith from first to last." But this phrase can be understood better in light of Rom 3:22: "God's righteousness coming through Christ's faithfulness for all who have faith" (my translation). What Paul says in Rom 1:17 is that God's righteousness is revealed from Christ's faithfulness and effective to all who have faith. His point is that we may be set right with God and become children of God through Christ's faithfulness. It is not by my faith in Christ but rather Christ's faithfulness that makes me a child of God. This means Christians must participate in Christ's faithfulness, dying to sin and living to God. Thus Paul says, quoting Hab 2:4, "The righteous one will live by faith" (my translation). Paul's main concern is not with how one can be saved or justified but rather with how one can live faithfully (cf. Gal 5:6).

Excursus: Faith/Faithfulness in Rom 3:21–26

The threefold nature of faithfulness is at the heart of Rom 3:21–26.[11] In this passage, Paul explains how God's righteousness (or God's faithfulness) came into the world and how people can participate in it. This passage is complex and difficult to understand because the Greek genitive phrases involved are ambiguous. The genitive has an "A of B" structure, such as, "the righteousness of God" and "the faith of Christ." Many commentators interpret these phrases as "objective genitives." According to that interpretation, God justifies the one who has faith *in* Jesus. But I take these genitive phrases as "subjective genitives," in which case "the righteousness of God" means God's righteousness and "the faith of Christ" means Christ's faithfulness.[12] Next is my revised translation of Rom 3:21–26 (italics indicate my translation):

But now, apart from law, *God's righteousness* has been disclosed, and is attested by the law and the prophets, *God's righteousness through the faithfulness of Jesus Christ for all who have faith*. For there is no distinction, since all have sinned and fall short of the glory of God; they are now justified by his grace as a gift, through the redemption that is in Christ Jesus, whom God put forward as *a mercy seat for reconciliation* by his blood, effective through faith. He did this to show his righteousness, because in his divine forbearance he had passed over the sins previously committed; it was to prove at the present time that he himself is righteous and that he justifies the one who has *the faithfulness of Jesus*.

---

11. Threefold faithfulness is shown in 1 Cor 1:9: "God is faithful; by him you were called into the fellowship of his Son, Jesus Christ our Lord." God's faithfulness as a theme is consistent throughout Paul's letters. God sent his Son and proved his love for us (Rom 5; 8). God calls his people in the grace of Christ (Gal 1:6). Christ was faithful to God. He was crucified because of his faithfulness. But God raised him from the dead (2 Cor 13:4). Followers of Jesus must also be faithful and imitate Christ (1 Cor 3:11).

12. Richard Hays, "PISTIS and Pauline Christology: What Is at Stake?," in *Pauline Theology*, ed. E. Elizabeth Johnson and David M. Hay (Atlanta: Scholars Press, 1997), 35–60, 53. See also Richard Hays, *The Faith of Jesus Christ: The Narrative Substructure of Galatians 3:1–4:11* (Grand Rapids: Eerdmans, 2002), 141–62. See also Luke Timothy Johnson, "Rom 3:21–26 and the Faith of Jesus," CBQ 44, no. 1 (1982): 77–90.

We can see a chiasm in this passage, and the focal idea is in v. 24–25a:[13]

A 3:21–22 But now, God's righteousness has been disclosed through Jesus's faithfulness for all who have faith

B 3:23 All have sinned and fall short of the glory of God

C 3:24–25a They are now justified by his grace as a gift, through the redemption that is in Christ Jesus, whom God put forward as a mercy seat for reconciliation

B' 3:25b God dealt with the sins previously committed and showed his covenantal love

A' 3:26 At the present time, it was to prove that God is righteous; God justifies those who have Jesus's faithfulness

A 3:21–22

Dia pisteos Iesou Christou in 3:22 is usually translated as "through faith in Jesus Christ" (NIV, NRSV, NKJ). But it can also be rendered as "through the faithfulness of Jesus Christ" (CEB). In the former, faith is the believer's, but in the latter, faith is Christ's. The latter makes better sense because if Paul meant "faith in Christ," the phrase "for all who believe" would be redundant. Moreover, if he had meant "believer's faith in Christ," he could have used a clearer phrase like this: *pistis en christo*, which does not involve the genitive case. If he used this phrase with the preposition *en*, which means "in," we can say unambiguously *pistis en christo* denotes believer's faith in Christ. Interestingly, in post-Pauline letters, we see the prepositional phrase "faith in Christ." For example, 1 Tim 3:13 has *en pistei te en christo iesou*, "the faith that is in Christ Jesus" (also 2 Tim 1:13). Also, 2 Tim 3:15 confirms this "faith in Christ": "How from childhood you have known the sacred writings that are able to instruct you for salvation *through faith in Christ Jesus* [*dia pisteos te en christo iesou*]" (italics mine). Technically, the Greek genitive can mean either "faith

13. Kim, *Rereading Romans*, 37–38.

in Christ" or "faithfulness of Christ." But given the previous comparison and the flow of ideas in Rom 3:21–22, the more natural reading is that God's righteousness was revealed from Christ's faithfulness to all who believe. A similar pattern of this idea is seen in Rom 1:17, as we saw before: "from faith to faith."

B 3:23

The idea of B that "all have sinned and fall short of the glory of God" (Rom 3:23) refers to Rom 1:18–3:20, where Paul talks about the hopeless human situation in which all people were unfaithful to God. Here, Paul reminds his audience of where they were before receiving the grace of Christ.

C 3:24–25a

C is the central unit in the chiasm. Here, Paul specifies Christ's work and his faithfulness, and he explains how one can be set right with God. Believers' justification (or being set right with God) is possible "by his grace as a gift, through the redemption that is in Christ Jesus" (Rom 3:24). Jesus's grace means he devoted his life to demonstrating God's righteousness or his justice. He was crucified because of his challenge to imperial justice and all forms of evil in society. If he had proclaimed the gospel of peace and prosperity, he would have been welcomed by Rome and would not have been executed. Jesus's grace means his gracious work and love for God's righteousness. Jesus broke the chains of evil and showed God's righteousness in the world. Those who appreciate his love feel the grace of God. They are empowered to live with Christ's love. They are restored to the love of God. Even though they are still in the world, being under the dominance of the empire, they know God is more powerful and wiser than the world. They feel freedom in Christ and are engaged in the world to show God's love in Christ. The redemption (*apolutrosis*) in Christ means they now see a new world of hope in God and participate in the work of Christ.

Then, in Rom 3:25, Paul comments on how God sent Jesus "as a mercy seat for reconciliation [*hilasterion*]" (my translation). The typical translation of *hilasterion* is "a sacrifice of atonement" (NRSV and NIV) or "a propitiation" (KJV), which evokes the image of Yom Kippur (the Day of Atonement). On the Day of Atonement, animal blood was sprinkled on the cover of the ark of the covenant, called *kaporeth*, which is translated as hilasterion in the Septuagint. With this image, Jesus is considered the place of atonement (like the "mercy seat" in Heb 9:5) or the means of sacrifice (so "a propitiation"). In Greek culture, hilasterion usually refers to propitiation, which means to placate an angry god.[14] But I would propose that hilasterion means "a mercy seat for reconciliation." As God appears on the gold cover of the ark on Yom Kippur, so also he appears in Jesus, who demonstrated God's righteousness and reconciles those who come to God through him. It must be noted that what God is presenting is not Jesus's death but Jesus in the fullness of his life, which implies that what God considers important is not only Jesus's death (as "propitiation" would suggest) but his life as a whole, including his death.[15] "By his blood, effective through faith" indicates Jesus's price for demonstrating God's righteousness. Here "through faith" must be "Jesus's faithfulness," given the statement in Rom 3:22 that God's righteousness has been disclosed through Jesus's faithfulness.[16] What Paul is trying to

14. The idea of propitiation seems a bit weird because of how a righteous God allows his innocent Son to be tortured and killed at the hands of evil. Here the issue is the wrath of God that needs to be dealt with. There are other ideas of atonement: (1) expiation as a cost for mending a broken relationship between God and humanity; (2) ransom theory that God pays a ransom price to the devil; (3) penal-substitution theory that deals with punishment through Jesus's vicarious death; (4) satisfaction theory that meets the highest moral demand of God through the perfect, sinless sacrifice of Jesus; and (5) Jesus's death as a righteous suffering for demonstrating God's rule in the world. As we see here, Jesus's act of giving himself is a matter of interpretation. For more atonement ideas, see Reasoner, *Romans in Full Circle*, 23–41. See also Mark Allan Powell, *Fortress Introduction to the Gospels*, 2nd ed. (Minneapolis: Fortress, 2019), 89–91.

15. David Brondos, *Paul on the Cross: Reconstructing the Apostle's Story of Redemption* (Minneapolis: Fortress, 2006), 63–190.

16. Bruce Longenecker, "PISTIS in Romans 3:25: Neglected Evidence for the Faithfulness of Christ," *New Testament Studies* 39 (1993): 478–80. See also Charles Talbert, *Romans* (Macon, GA: Smyth & Helwys, 2002), 107, 110. Otherwise, it would be awkward to insert God's faith

say here is that God considered Jesus himself, not his death, as a mercy seat for reconciliation because of his faithfulness.[17] God's love and justice were displayed publicly by Jesus, who was obedient to God's will.[18]

B' 3:25b

This chiasm unit deals with the hopeless human predicament. God dealt with the sins previously committed and showed his righteousness, which is covenantal love. God decided to deal with the past this way to open a new path of reconciliation through Jesus.

A' 3:26

This chiasm unit refers to 3:21–22 (A), which deals with God's righteousness coming through Christ's faithfulness for all who have faith. In this unit, the emphasis is to prove that God is righteous. God is righteous because now he justifies those who come to him through Jesus's faithfulness. As Rom 3:26 reads, "It was to prove at the present time that he himself is righteous and that he justifies the one who has *the faithfulness of Jesus*" (italics indicate my translation).

Galatians

In Galatians, Paul argues that God is faithful because he is loyal to his covenant made with Abraham and extends his love to all. As Gal 3:8 notes, "And the scripture, foreseeing that God would justify the gentiles by faith, declared the gospel beforehand to Abraham, saying, 'All the gentiles shall be blessed in you.'" God fulfilled this promise through Christ's faithfulness. All people are justified through Christ Jesus's faithfulness (*dia pisteos christou Iesou*), not by "the works of the law" (Gal 2:16a; *erga nomou*). That is, what makes one stand in

---

or a believer's faith along with Jesus's blood. See Richard Longenecker, *The Epistle to the Romans* (Grand Rapids: Eerdmans, 2016), 388–469.

17. Johnson, *Reading Romans*, 61. See also Longenecker, *Epistle to the Romans*, 388–469.

18. Jesus's obedient faith is seen in Rom 5:12–21 (cf. Phil 2:6–11). See also Louis Martyn, "A Law-Observant Messiah to the Gentiles," *Scottish Journal of Theology* 38 (1985): 307–24.

good relationship with God is not circumcision or observing dietary laws but rather following the way of Christ through his faithfulness and spirit. Justification does not need strings attached other than genuine faith after Christ's example. This point is explicated in Gal 2:16b: "And we have come to believe in [eis, 'into'] Christ Jesus, so that we might be justified by *the faithfulness of Christ* [*pisteos christou*], and not by doing the works of the law, because no one will be justified by the works of the law" (italics indicate my translation). Here again, we see that the Greek genitive case *pisteos christou* must be the subjective genitive (Christ's faithfulness) in order to make sense in context.[19] Furthermore, in the injunction "believe in [eis] Christ Jesus," the preposition *eis* denotes an action (into). The implication is that the believer is to participate "into" Christ's faith. In the end, Paul confesses his faith about Christ. In fact, he talks about Christ's faith, which must be his. Because Christ lives in him, he now lives by Christ's faith.

The phrase "not by the works of the law" does not mean that the law is wrong or outdated. Paul affirms the validity of the law in Rom 7:12. The law is holy and cannot be overthrown by faith (Rom 3:31). Paul clearly says the law is not opposed to God's promise: "Is the law then opposed to the promises of God? Certainly not! For if a law had been given that could make alive, then righteousness would indeed come through the law" (Gal 3:21). Rather, Paul believes that the law came after faith and that, as a result, it should be informed by faith, which is in God and in Christ (Gal 3:17–19). The eye of faith looks at God's promise given to Abraham and its fulfillment with Jesus. For Paul, the problem is those who stick to the law and limit God's promise. As a result, they do not see the importance of faith and Christ's fulfillment of the law.

19. See Kim, *Rereading Galatians*, 26. *Pistis christou* appears in the following: Gal 2:16, 20; 3:22; Rom 3:22, 25–26; Phil 3:9. As we read Abraham's faith in Rom 4:16, it is natural to read this phrase *pistis christou* as Christ's faithfulness. Jesus's obedient faith is seen in Phil 2:6–11 and Rom 5:12–21. Similarly, Louis Martyn sees Christ's faithfulness in Gal 2:16–20 as his faithful death. See Martyn, "Law-Observant Messiah," 307–24.

SUMMARY

The writers of the New Testament understand faith in a variety of ways. In Hebrews, faith is conviction, assurance, or hope about the God-given future. As Heb 11:1 says, "Now faith is the assurance of things hoped for, the conviction of things not seen." Here "faith" means conviction about the future. No matter what happens, one must trust God and not give in to the challenges of the present age. Certainly, this aspect of faith is desperately needed in times of turmoil. But at other times, other aspects of faith are also needed. The book of James emphasizes both faith and works. Faith and works are inseparable in James. It is likely that the church to which James writes misunderstood Paul's teaching about faith and began believing that faith could be separated from works. But Paul never separates faith from works (deeds). What counts is "faith working through love" (Gal 5:6). As James says in 2:21–26, faith without works is dead:

> Was not our ancestor Abraham justified by works when he offered his son Isaac on the altar? You see that faith was active along with his works, and faith was brought to completion by the works. Thus the scripture was fulfilled that says, "Abraham believed God, and it was reckoned to him as righteousness," and he was called the friend of God. You see that a person is justified by works and not by faith alone. Likewise, was not Rahab the prostitute also justified by works when she welcomed the messengers and sent them out by another road? For just as the body without the spirit is dead, so faith without works is also dead.

In the post-Pauline letters (mostly in the Deutero-Pauline and Pastorals), we see still more understandings of faith. After Paul, and in response to the many false teachers influencing his churches, faith is understood as a set of teachings about Jesus. These false teachers brought radical Gnosticism or religious syncretism into the church. In this context, correct teaching is the aspect of faith that needs to be emphasized.

For this reason, we see the use of the phrase "faith in Christ" (*pistis en christo*).[20]

But Paul's view of faith is different from other letters. He emphasizes God's faithfulness, Christ's faithfulness, and Christian participatory faith. Faith is not knowledge but loyalty to God and to Christ. It is vibrant living for God's righteousness through Jesus.

QUESTIONS FOR REFLECTION

1. Why are there so many different aspects of faith in the New Testament? Do we also need diverse aspects of faith today? What is the benefit of taking faith from the perspective of the Deutero-Pauline and Pastoral letters? What are the limitations?

2. Is there a way that Christians engage other religious people with Christian faith?

3. How can we live our faith in a capitalist system? How can we practice holistic faith in our world?

20. Kim, "Reclaiming Christ's Body," 20–29. See also Yung Suk Kim, "Between Text and Sermon: Hebrews 11:8–16," *Interpretation* 72, no. 2 (2018): 204–6.

6

FREEDOM

OVERVIEW

Freedom or liberation is an important topic of the Bible and goes back to the story of Exodus. The Israelites were in slavery to Egypt, and God heard their cries for justice and liberation. He sent Moses to free them from the enslaving conditions of life in Egypt. Initially, Moses was hesitant to go there, but God assured him that he would be with him and that his brother, Aaron, would help him. After gaining their freedom from the Egyptians, the Israelites were led out into the wilderness, to what they thought would be their promised land. But their expectations were not matched by harsh living conditions in the desert. They were freed from Egyptian slavery, but they still had a long way to go to reach the promised land. As the narrative of the exodus from Egypt transitions to the narrative of the conquest of Canaan, the formerly oppressed Hebrews become the oppressors. While we do not know what exactly happened to the Israelites, historically speaking, the conquest narrative reveals the irony of their liberation.

As we see previously, freedom has three aspects: (1) freedom *from* external conditions of life such as slavery, oppression, or poverty; (2) freedom *for* something such as building a new community of love; and (3) freedom *in* someone such as God. We see these aspects of freedom in the New Testament.[1]

Jesus worked to liberate people from the rule of evil power and empire and introduced the rule of God in the here and now. While he was not a revolutionary, he freed those who were tormented by demons, healed the sick from their diseases, and provided food to those who were hungry. He made disciples so that they could build a new community of love, justice, and peace. Jesus also teaches that freedom should be guided by God's will. He obeyed God's will and walked the path of faith until he died. Paul also talks about three kinds of freedom: "freedom from something; freedom for something; freedom in God/Christ."[2] For example, in Romans, he talks about freedom from sin or the law of sin. As Jesus won the fight against sin, his followers must do the same. They have to put to death the deeds of the body by the Spirit (Rom 8:13). As they are free in Christ, they must use their freedom to build a new community of love. Their freedom must be guided by the Spirit, and they must follow the way of Christ.

GRECO-ROMAN AND JEWISH TEXTS AND CONTEXTS

During the Roman Empire, freedom was limited. People in Roman-occupied lands were controlled by the government and local officials. They were free to worship their gods, but they were not free to speak or to act against the government.[3] Slaves were commodities, and even free people had to live in a chain of benefaction on top of which the emperor stood. Sedition against the empire meant death.

In this time of imperial society, freedom is internalized and applied to the mind or heart only. Stoicism emphasizes

---

1. Kim, *Preaching the New Testament*, 37–73.

2. Kim, 37–73.

3. According to Emperor Trajan's response to Pliny, he forbids the formation of a group of firefighters and limits the freedom of assembly. See Pliny, *Letters*, Attalus, accessed September 28, 2020, 10.34, https://tinyurl.com/y3fje6tz.

apatheia, which means a status without suffering (freedom from passions). This status is limited to the mind. Regardless of external pains and privations, a person must maintain peace of mind without being controlled by outer forces or inner passions. While this philosophy offers aid to those living in chaos due to personal or social disasters, it does not address the causes of disasters. True peace of mind requires justice. If one has to endure hardships or injustices without addressing their causes, how could true peace of mind be achieved? If pain does not have a purpose, how can it be endured? In this sense, *apatheia* is an easy, temporary medicine that may relieve a person's suffering. But Stoics do not deal with injustices or the needless suffering inflicted on the marginalized. They do not know how to deal with suffering or pain other than by trying to avoid them. The Roman Stoic philosopher Seneca does not realize the seriousness of pain itself and thinks that pain is easily controlled. He says, "Pain is slight if opinion has added nothing to it; . . . in thinking it slight, you will make it slight. Everything depends on opinion; ambition, luxury, greed, hark back to opinion. It is according to opinion that we suffer. . . . So let us also win the way to victory in all our struggles,—for the reward is . . . virtue, steadfastness of soul, and a peace that is won for all time."[4] Controlling all emotions is not always bad because humans need to express what they feel and find solutions. But Stoics do not see the healthy function of emotion or passion. They think that passions or emotions are bad, and as a result, they do not deal with social ills or injustices. They do not question unjust social structures.

In the Jewish world in the first century CE, Pharisees emphasized freedom from impurity and idolatry because they were concerned with Jewish laws. They did not concern themselves with gaining freedom from political empires or oppression. The Zealots sought freedom from foreign powers through armed revolt, while the Sadducees were largely

---

4. Seneca, *Epistles*, Stoic Therapy, accessed September 28, 2020, lxxviii, 13–16, https://tinyurl.com/y2be9cf9.

indifferent to political or social freedom because they bene-
fited from their cooperation with Rome. The Essenes withdrew to the desert and in so doing freed themselves from
both the corrupt politics of Rome and the corrupt religion
of Jerusalem.

FREEDOM IN PAUL'S LETTERS

"Free from the Law"

In Paul's view, the law is not useless or outdated because of
Christ. In Romans, Paul vehemently affirms that the law is
good. The law is holy (Rom 7:12), and faith cannot nullify it
(Rom 3:30). He never says that the law is an imperfect means
of justification because people cannot keep it perfectly. The
issue, for Paul, is not the existence of the law but the misun-
derstanding of it. The law can become an obstacle to freedom
or to justification if it is absolutized or misunderstood. The
law does not precede faith. Abraham's faith came before
the law. And even faith does not precede the grace of God,
as he says in Gal 2:21, "I do not nullify the grace of God; for if
justification comes through the law, then Christ died for
nothing." By his grace, God called Abraham out of nowhere.
If the law is absolutized with zeal, there is no room for faith,
which is to respond to God's call and promise. More importantly, Paul's argument is that Jesus Christ exemplified the
purpose of the law, as he says in Rom 10:4, "Christ is the end
[telos] of the law." This means the law must be reinterpreted
through Christ and his love of the neighbor. As Paul writes
in Rom 13:8–10, "Owe no one anything, except to love one
another; for the one who loves another has fulfilled the law.
The commandments, 'You shall not commit adultery; You
shall not murder; You shall not steal; You shall not covet'; and
any other commandment, are summed up in this word, 'Love
your neighbor as yourself.' Love does no wrong to a neighbor; therefore, love is the fulfilling of the law." Because of
the previous concerns about the law, he talks to the Roman
Christians about his gospel of faith and the Spirit and asks

them to be "free from the law" through a marriage metaphor in Rom 7:3–6. Here, his point is not that Christ killed
the law or replaced it but that now is a new age, one in which
Christ has fulfilled the law. If people absolutize the law without grasping what Christ did in fulfilling it, they are slaves
"under the old written code" (Rom 7:6). Paul exhorts them to
see the new life of the Spirit from Christ.

How can one be free from the law? The answer is found
in Rom 7:4 and Gal 2:19. Rom 7:4 reads, "In the same way, my
friends, *you have died to the law through the body of Christ, so
that you may belong to another*, to him who has been raised
from the dead in order that we may bear fruit for God" (italics mine). Here "through the body of Christ" must be Christ's
body crucified. So "dying to the law through the body of
Christ" means that one should know the meaning of Christ's
crucifixion and live as he did, not letting the law be an absolute in one's life. Jesus did not view the law as the Pharisees
did. He interpreted the law radically with a focus on the love
of neighbor, especially God's love of the marginalized, sinners, and tax collectors. He even broke some parts of the law
in the eyes of the Pharisees. He healed the sick on the Sabbath but insisted that he did not break the law because the
Sabbath was made for humans, not humans for the Sabbath
(Mark 2:27–28). However, far from being morally lax, Jesus
commends the law, as he says in Matt 5:18–20, "For truly I tell
you, until heaven and earth pass away, not one letter, not one
stroke of a letter, will pass from the law until all is accomplished. Therefore, whoever breaks one of the least of these
commandments, and teaches others to do the same, will
be called least in the kingdom of heaven; but whoever does
them and teaches them will be called great in the kingdom
of heaven. For I tell you, unless your righteousness exceeds
that of the scribes and Pharisees, you will never enter the
kingdom of heaven." But Jesus's thoroughness is based on a
deeper reinterpretation of the law, as Matt 5:38–48 reads,

"You have heard that it was said, 'An eye for an eye and a tooth
for a tooth.' But I say to you, Do not resist an evildoer. But if

anyone strikes you on the right cheek, turn the other also; and if anyone wants to sue you and take your coat, give your cloak as well; and if anyone forces you to go one mile, go also the second mile. Give to everyone who begs from you, and do not refuse anyone who wants to borrow from you.

"You have heard that it was said, 'You shall love your neighbor and hate your enemy.' But I say to you, Love your enemies and pray for those who persecute you, so that you may be children of your Father in heaven; for he makes his sun rise on the evil and on the good, and sends rain on the righteous and on the unrighteous. For if you love those who love you, what reward do you have? Do not even the tax collectors do the same? And if you greet only your brothers and sisters, what more are you doing than others? Do not even the gentiles do the same? Be perfect, therefore, as your heavenly Father is perfect."

Like Rom 7:4, Gal 2:19 also gives us the answer to the question of how one can be free from the law: "For through the law I died to the law, so that I might live to God. I have been crucified with Christ." While we interpreted "through the body of Christ" in Rom 7:4 as Christ's crucifixion, the phrase "through the law" here is far more puzzling. But given the overall argument in Romans, this phrase likely means "the law of God," as Paul says later in Romans: "For I delight in *the law of God* in my inmost self" (Rom 7:22; italics mine); "Thanks be to God through Jesus Christ our Lord! So then, with my mind I am a slave to *the law of God*, but with my flesh I am a slave to the law of sin" (Rom 7:25; italics mine). So "the law of God" in these verses means all that God wants: righteousness, peace, life, and joy. "Through the law" also may refer to Rom 8:2: "For *the law of the Spirit of life in Christ Jesus* has set you free from the law of sin and of death" (italics mine).

"Freed from Sin or the Law of Sin"

More fundamentally, one needs to be free not from the law per se but from sin or from the law of sin. That idea is prevalent in Rom 6–8 and a few related texts:

Rom 6:7–8

For whoever has died is *freed from sin*. But if we have died with Christ, we believe that we will also live with him. (italics mine)

Rom 6:10

The death he died, he died to sin, once for all; but the life he lives, he lives to God.

Rom 6:17–18

But thanks be to God that you, having once been *slaves of sin*, have become obedient from the heart to the form of teaching to which you were entrusted, *and that you, having been set free from sin, have become slaves of righteousness*. (italics mine)

Rom 6:22

But now that you have been *freed from sin* and enslaved to God, the advantage you get is sanctification. The end is eternal life. (italics mine)

Rom 7:23–25

But I see in my members another law at war with the law of my mind, making me captive to the law of sin that dwells in my members. Wretched man that I am! Who will rescue me from this body of death? Thanks be to God through Jesus Christ our Lord! So then, with my mind I am *a slave to the law of God, but with my flesh I am a slave to the law of sin*. (italics mine)

Rom 8:1–4

There is therefore now no condemnation for those who are in Christ Jesus. *For the law of the Spirit of life in Christ Jesus has set you free from the law of sin and of death*. For God has done what the law, weakened by the flesh, could not do: by sending his own Son in the likeness of sinful flesh, and to deal with sin, he condemned sin in the flesh, so that the just requirement of the law might be fulfilled in us, who walk not according to the flesh but according to the Spirit. (italics mine)

In the previous texts, we notice that freedom from sin or the law of sin does not mean that one is free to do anything. Freedom in these passages means one's commitment to God and to living with Christ. In Rom 6:7, the one who died with Christ is freed from sin and will continue to live with him. If one died with Christ, sin does not reign on him or her. Dying with Christ means to follow the way of Christ, which defeated the power of sin by dying to sin, as indicated in Rom 6:10: "The death he died, he died to sin, once for all; but the life he lives, he lives to God." Jesus's dying to sin means he was not ruled by it and that he followed the will of God. Because of this, God made him live. He lives to God now. Likewise, dying with Christ means to live a Christlike life. It means to put to death the deeds of the body by the Spirit (Rom 8:13). It means to be led by the Spirit and to live according to the Spirit. To die with Christ is to follow Jesus continuously. Thus dying with Christ is not an abstract concept in that one dies with Christ existentially or in a mysterious spiritual sense. As Paul says in Rom 6:17–18, "But thanks be to God that you, having once been *slaves of sin*, have become obedient from the heart to the form of teaching to which you were entrusted, *and that you, having been set free from sin, have become slaves of righteousness*" (italics mine). Christ's followers changed their allegiance from sin to righteousness or to God (Rom 6:22). Paul expresses his thanks for this new life in God through Christ: "Thanks be to God through Jesus Christ our Lord! So then, with my mind I am *a slave to the law of God, but with my flesh I am a slave to the law of sin*" (Rom 7:25; italics mine). Here, freedom means to obey God, to follow the law of God, which is interchangeable with all things God wants: righteousness, peace, life, and joy. In Rom 8:1–2, Paul declares that "there is therefore now no condemnation for those who are in Christ Jesus. *For the law of the Spirit of life in Christ Jesus has set you free from the law of sin and of death*" (italics mine). One finds peace with God by following "the law of the Spirit of life in Christ Jesus," which means to follow the Spirit and Christ. If one is not led by the Spirit or Christ, one is led by the law of sin.

In Paul's thinking, there is no neutral road, no third way. He is worried that sin seizes an opportunity in the law, as he says in Rom 7:8: "But sin, seizing an opportunity in the commandment, produced in me all kinds of covetousness. Apart from the law sin lies dead." The solution is to accept the grace of God through Christ (Rom 5:21) and not let sin exercise dominion in our bodies (Rom 6:12), which means to put to death the deeds of the body by the Spirit (Rom 8:13).

"Freedom for Something"

Freedom in Christ does not mean that one can do anything in Christ. Freedom has a purpose. In the Corinthian church, there were some who thought that "all things are lawful" (1 Cor 6:12; 10:23). But Paul's response is, "Not all things are beneficial. . . . I will not be dominated by anything" (1 Cor 6:12). "Not all things build up" (1 Cor 10:23). Some in the Corinthian church were engaged in immorality and were careless with their bodies. Paul says they were bought with a price, and therefore, they had to glorify God in their body (1 Cor 6:20). Some in the Corinthian church thought they knew correctly about food sacrificed to idols. That is, they can eat anything because food is clean and no idol truly exists in the world. Because there is only one true God, food is food. While Paul agrees with this idea, he does not agree with their attitude, which does not care about the weak consciences of others (1 Cor 8:7–8). His conclusion is that "knowledge puffs up, but love builds up" (1 Cor 8:1). So he advises the Corinthians not to exercise their freedom irresponsibly, as he says in 1 Cor 8:9–13:

> But take care that this liberty of yours does not somehow become a stumbling block to the weak. For if others see you, who possess knowledge, eating in the temple of an idol, might they not, since their conscience is weak, be encouraged to the

point of eating food sacrificed to idols? So by your knowledge those weak believers for whom Christ died are destroyed. But when you thus sin against members of your family, and wound their conscience when it is weak, you sin against Christ. Therefore, if food is a cause of their falling, I will never eat meat, so that I may not cause one of them to fall.

In 1 Cor 12–14, Paul deals with the issues of spiritual gifts, noting that some in the church did not exercise their gifts responsibly. He implores the Corinthians to use their gifts carefully in order to build up the church rather than to boast about themselves (cf. Gal 5:13). He writes, "Those who speak in a tongue build up themselves, but those who prophesy build up the church" (1 Cor 14:4). He does not want people to speak unintelligible words before other members (1 Cor 14:9). He says, "Nevertheless, in church I would rather speak five words with my mind, in order to instruct others also, than ten thousand words in a tongue" (1 Cor 14:19).

For Paul, freedom also has to do with proclaiming the gospel. In 1 Cor 9, Paul says he uses his freedom to proclaim the gospel. He has rights to use as an apostle, but he does not use them. These rights likely include provisions of food and drink, financial gifts, and the ability to travel with a partner. But he says he did not use any of these rights so as not to burden people (1 Cor 9:15–16). Instead, he worked hard night and day (1 Thess 2:9), and when he received financial gifts from others, he did not depend on people within the church while he was in a particular region. Why? The answer is found in 1 Cor 9:19–23:

For though I am free with respect to all, I have made myself a slave to all, so that I might win more of them. To the Jews I became as a Jew, in order to win Jews. To those under the law I became as one under the law (though I myself am not under the law) so that I might win those under the law. To those outside the law I became as one outside the law (though I am not free from God's law but am under Christ's law) so that I might win those outside the law. To the weak I became weak, so that I might win the weak. I have become all things to all people, that I might by all means save some. I do it all for the sake of the gospel, so that I may share in its blessings.

"Freedom for something" also means one must maintain their freedom. As Paul says in Gal 5:1, "For freedom Christ has set us free. Stand firm, therefore, and do not submit again to a yoke of slavery." The freed Galatians must not return to the old way of life. In other words, they should not turn to the different gospel that demands circumcision for the gentiles.

"Freedom in Someone"

Because Christ set us free from the present evil age (Gal 1:4), our freedom should be rooted in his work. We should follow Christ as Christ followed God's will. When we are not led by the Spirit or rooted in the way of Christ, we, like the Israelites who left slavery in Egypt only to become conquerors in Canaan, may become oppressors of others. According to Paul, Christians need to renew their spirit constantly by reminding themselves of what Christ has done and why he gave his life for them. The foundation of the church is Christ (1 Cor 3:11). All Christian works must be built on that foundation. In the end, in Christ, "the only thing that counts is faith working through love" (Gal 5:6).

SUMMARY

As we have seen, there are three aspects of freedom: freedom from something, freedom for something, and freedom in someone. It is important to distinguish between Christian freedom in Paul's letters and freedom discourse in the Greco-Roman and Jewish texts and contexts. For while Stoics emphasize the virtue of self-control and inner peace of mind, they do not address oppression or injustice. But in Paul's view, the whole world is God's domain and as such requires freedom from injustices. For him, freedom means entering God's domain by leaving the way of sin. One should seek the righteousness of God by following Jesus and being guided by the Spirit.

Paul's talk of "free from the law, sin, or the law of sin" needs to be discussed in context. He does not reject the law per se or Judaism. He problematizes the use of the law by Jews who do not accept Jesus as the Messiah (Christ), especially in the context of Galatians and Romans. For Paul, the issue is a matter of priority. As grace stands before and above faith, so too does faith precede the law. As Christ fulfilled the law through his faithfulness, so too do Christians experience freedom—even freedom from the law—when they follow Christ.

In Paul's view, the enemy is not the law but rather sin working through the law. Much of Rom 6–8 is concerned with the power the sin exercises in human living and the means of breaking free from that power. Paul describes this freedom from sin in various ways: "dying with Christ," "being baptized into his death," "following the law of the Spirit," "by the Spirit putting to death the deeds of the body."

Christian freedom should be used carefully to edify the community of God, and followers of Jesus must remember Christ who is the foundation of the *ekklesia*. Freedom in Christ does not mean one can do anything (1 Cor 8–11). "Knowledge puffs up, but love builds up" (1 Cor 8:1). Spiritual gifts need to be used for supporting one another in community. Freedom should be used for the gospel of Christ (1 Cor 9). It is not for self-indulgence (Gal 5:13). Freedom should be maintained at all costs (Gal 5:1).

For Paul, Christian freedom must be based on the way of God and Christ. Christians must know what God wants and commit themselves to doing it. Likewise, they must know what Jesus Christ did and why he gave himself for them. Christians must be guided by the Spirit and submit to the way of God and Christ. Otherwise, they may fall in the trap of boasting about themselves, ignoring others' needs, or even becoming oppressors themselves.

QUESTIONS FOR REFLECTION

1. Let us talk about various notions of freedom in our day. What kind of freedom is necessary for our lives? Include personal, communal, and social dimensions.

2. What do you say about the three aspects of freedom?

3. Evaluate the "household codes" (Col 3:18–4:1; Eph 5:21–6:9; Titus 2:1–10; and 1 Pet 2:18–3:7) where freedom is severely limited. What is the role of these codes in ancient churches?

7

NEW LIFE / NEW CREATION

OVERVIEW

Paul's view of new life is different from the Greco-Roman world. Stoics teach the virtue of self-control with which people can survive in a harsh world. Their teaching solidifies the current system of political and social hierarchy. The good life is simply to conform to the current system and find peace within the self. But Paul envisions radical change both for the world and for the self, brought about by God's love and Christ's grace. Members of the church live a new life in Christ, gathering together to praise God, remembering Christ's sacrifice, and loving one another. They are filled with love, hope, and faith and are able to endure difficulties in the world because they have hope in God. They do not retaliate against evildoers. They struggle with the harsh realities in the world and yet enjoy their new life in Christ.

"New life / new creation" is the part of the gospel in which God's righteousness is revealed. The gospel is "the power of God for salvation to everyone who has faith" (Rom 1:16). In other words, the power of God is not the power to destroy but the power to give "new life" in Christ. God's power saves people from chaos and darkness. Those who participate in Christ will begin to experience new life in him. But living this new life requires an ongoing response to God's faithfulness and Jesus's faithfulness. Eventually, new life / new creation will be completed on the Parousia when God restores his creation.

GRECO-ROMAN AND JEWISH
TEXTS AND CONTEXTS

"New life" is defined as a new meaning of life, a new form of personal, communal life and a hope-filled future. In Paul's time, the Roman Empire tried to communicate its imperial gospel to the people and told them they would be happy with imperial peace and security. But that gospel did not provide them an authentic vision of a new life, one of respect, care, and justice. While ruling elites of the Roman world may have possessed these things, most people in the empire did not. This created huge disparities in society. Some people turned to mystery religions to meet their needs.[1] The rituals of the mystery cults provided followers with a sense of who they were and where they should have gone. For example, Isis, the goddess of fertility, listens to people who need "comfort, hopes, and encouragement in their hopeless situations."[2] The inscription of aretalogies reads,

> *I am Isis, the lord of every land . . .*
> *I gave and ordained laws for men, which no one is able to*
>   *change.*
> *I am eldest daughter of Kronos. I am wife and sister of King*
>   *Osiris . . .*
> *I divided the earth from the heaven. I showed the paths of*
>   *the stars . . .*
> *I brought together woman and man . . .*
> *I broke down the governments of tyrants . . .*
> *I established penalties for those who practice injustice.*
> *I decreed mercy to suppliants. With me the right prevails . . .*
> *I set free these in bonds.*[3]

1. Morton Smith, "Prolegomena to a Discussion of Aretalogies, Divine Men, the Gospels, and Jesus," JBL 90 (1971): 174–99. See also Howard Kee, "Aretalogy and Gospel," JBL 92 (1973): 402–22.

2. Yung Suk Kim, *Truth, Testimony, and Transformation: A New Reading of the "I Am" Sayings of Jesus in the Fourth Gospel* (Eugene, OR: Cascade, 2014), 20.

3. R. S. Kraemer, ed., *Maenads, Martyrs, Matrons, Monastics: A Sourcebook on Women's Religions in the Greco-Roman World* (Minneapolis: Fortress, 1998), 368–70. See also Rose

Isis has authority over humanity and the power to rule the world. Some people depend on her power and wisdom to find a new meaning of life. And because so many people in the ancient world lived under the unjust circumstances of social disparity, mystery religions were numerous.

Hellenistic Jews found a new meaning of life through their commitment to the law. They tried to be faithful to the law, especially the purity laws. While they were not isolationists, they were not interested in reforming society or correcting injustices. In Palestine, the Essenes secluded themselves from the world and founded their own community. They claimed that they were children of light and true heirs of prophets and priests. Their new life was based on sectarianism and asceticism. The Essenes claimed that new life came through them.

NEW LIFE / NEW CREATION IN PAUL'S LETTERS

For Paul, new life begins with justification, which means to be set right with God. This new relationship is possible through faith, which means to follow Jesus and his faithfulness. This faith is also trusting God and accepting his grace. New life in Christ grows over time. In other words, new life is not a onetime birth.[4] The language of "justification once and for all" needs to be reconsidered. Rather, new life is cultivated and sanctified through the way of Christ.

Hofman Arthur, *The Wisdom Goddess: Feminist Motifs in Eight Nag Hammadi Documents* (Lanham, MD: University Press of America, 1984), 161–62; Frank Trombley, "Prolegomena to the Systemic Analysis of Late Hellenistic Religion," in *Religious Writings and Religious Systems*, ed. J. Neusner and A. J. Levine (Atlanta: Scholars Press, 1989), 95–113. See also Satoko Yamaguchi, "'I Am' Sayings and Woman in Context," in *A Feminist Companion to John*, ed. Amy-Jill Levine (Sheffield: Sheffield Academic Press, 2003), 35–40.

4. In Jesus's encounter with Nicodemus (John 3), he says, "No one can see the kingdom of God without being born from above." He means that one needs to be born from above, implying a new life that depends on God from above. The Greek *anothen* has a double meaning: "again" or "from above." While Nicodemus thinks of it as a time of literal birth, Jesus means it metaphorically, emphasizing one's connection with God. See Yung Suk Kim's podcast, *Jesus and Nicodemus*, Anchor FM, March 23, 2020, https://tinyurl .com/y345ap9g.

"New Life" in Romans

In Romans, Paul develops the theme of new life as the letter progresses. In Rom 1:1–17 (the prologue of the letter), Paul talks about the gospel's power for salvation to everyone who has faith. The gospel creates new life for those who have faith—that is, for those who follow Jesus.

In Rom 1:18–3:20, Paul points out the universal problem of unfaithfulness to God and people's unwillingness to practice truth and justice. Here, Paul talks about the wrath of God that is caused by human unfaithfulness. He also argues that both Jews and gentiles failed to embody the truth of God. All have sinned and sought their glory and power. The Jews failed to embody the law of God, and the gentiles lived according to their passions. As a result, all are under the power of sin.

In Rom 3:21–4:25, Paul presents the solution to the wrath of God caused by human unfaithfulness. God's righteousness came through Christ's faithfulness for all who have faith. God justifies the one who has the faith of Jesus (Rom 3:26). Justification is accomplished through the law of faith, not by the works of the law. Since God is one, both Jews and gentiles are set right with God through the same faith. But faith cannot overthrow the law. The latter is fulfilled through the former. Then, in Rom 4:1–15, Paul connects faith to Abraham, who is the father of faith for all, both Jews and gentiles. Abraham was justified by his faithfulness. But before his justification, God called him. This call is the grace of God. Abraham responded to God's grace with faith. Here, faith is not a onetime yes but an ongoing loyalty or commitment to God.

In Rom 5:1–21, Paul says that while the benefit of justification is great, Jesus's followers will face suffering because of their new life in Christ. He assures his readers that God's love is excellent and that Christ's grace and faithfulness is the proof. The benefits of justification include peace with God, the assurance of God's love, and reconciliation with God. Yet Paul is not naive in thinking that these benefits will lead to peace with a world ruled by sin. He knows that conflicts will arise and that the world will oppose Christ's followers. Yet he also believes that Jesus's work and his grace are sufficient to reverse sin's work and rob it of its power.

In Rom 6:1–7:25, Paul takes pains to explain how to maintain new life in Christ. New life in Christ requires "dying to sin." He clearly says that Jesus's followers should not continue in sin because they received the grace of God (Rom 6:1–13). They died with Christ, which means their old self died to sin. "Dying to sin" means to no longer follow sinful passions. Sin's power may be undone when one overcomes its temptation and lives to God (Rom 6:9–10). As Christ died to sin, so also must his followers do the same. When they do, sin does not exercise dominion in their bodies (Rom 6:11–13). They are bound with God and may be sanctified and led to eternal life (Rom 6:19–23).

As Paul expands his description of new life in Christ, he focuses on "dying to the law." While the law is not sin, it may be used by sin (Rom 7:7–13). That is, when the law is absolutized without faith or love, sin has the opportunity to work through it. In this context, "dying to the law through the body of Christ" means, as we saw in the previous chapter, that one must know the meaning of Christ's crucifixion and live like him, not letting the law be absolutized in their life. Jesus did not view the law like the Pharisees. Rather, he interpreted the law radically, focusing on the love of neighbor and especially God's love of the marginalized, the sinners, and the tax collectors. He even broke the law in the eyes of the Pharisees. Paul's advice is to view the law as Jesus did. He thus implores his readers to follow "the law of God" rather than "the law of sin."

In Rom 8:1–39, Paul summarizes the new life in Christ that he discussed in Rom 5–7. On the one hand, he reassures Roman Christians that their new life in Christ is secure (Rom 8:1–4, 28–39). On the other hand, he implores them to be guided by the Spirit (Rom 8:5–11, 14–27). The conclusion is in Rom 8:12–13: "So then, brothers and sisters, we are debtors, not to the flesh, to live according to the flesh—for if you live according to the flesh, you will die; but if by the Spirit you put to death the deeds of the body, you will live." Rom 8 has the following chiastic structure:[5]

A 8:1–4 Assurance of new life in Christ Jesus

    B 8:5–11 New life by the spirit of God and of Jesus, not by the flesh

        C 8:12–13 By the Spirit put to death the deeds of the body, then you will live

    B 8:14–27 The role of the spirit of God for children of God

A 8:28–39 Assurance of the love of God in Christ

As seen previously, Paul emphasizes the maintenance of new life (C 8:12–13). To continue to live in the new life, Jesus's followers must continue to die with him, which means to kill sinful passions by the power of the Spirit. Most importantly, they have to trust God and Jesus. They have to believe that God's love is unchangeable and that Christ's grace is sufficient to deal with any issues.

However, this new life in Christ does not reject the place of Israel because God made a covenant with Abraham. Paul struggles to understand the slow response of Jews to Jesus. Yet he has hope that God will deal faithfully with his people: "O the depth of the riches and wisdom and knowledge of God! How unsearchable are his judgments and how inscrutable his ways! 'For who has known the mind of the Lord? Or who has been his counselor?' 'Or who has given a gift to him, to receive a gift in return?' For from him and through him and to him are all things. To him be the glory forever. Amen" (Rom 11:33–36).

New life in Christ continues to be discussed in 12:1–15:13. In this section, Paul talks about the new life of a community, based on mutual care and love. He asks people to be transformed by the renewing of their minds (Rom 12:2). He also asks them to be humble and to respect one another: "For by the grace given to me I say to everyone among you not to think

---

5. Kim, *Rereading Romans*, 63–70.

of yourself more highly than you ought to think, but to think with sober judgment, each according to the measure of faith that God has assigned" (Rom 12:3). In Rom 12:9–21, Paul gives a series of ethical codes to maintain a new life in Christ:

> Let love be genuine; hate what is evil, hold fast to what is good; love one another with mutual affection; outdo one another in showing honor. Do not lag in zeal, be ardent in spirit, serve the Lord. Rejoice in hope, be patient in suffering, persevere in prayer. Contribute to the needs of the saints; extend hospitality to strangers. Bless those who persecute you; bless and do not curse them. Rejoice with those who rejoice, weep with those who weep. Live in harmony with one another; do not be haughty, but associate with the lowly; do not claim to be wiser than you are. Do not repay anyone evil for evil, but take thought for what is noble in the sight of all. If it is possible, so far as it depends on you, live peaceably with all. Beloved, never avenge yourselves, but leave room for the wrath of God; for it is written, "Vengeance is mine, I will repay, says the Lord." No, "if your enemies are hungry, feed them; if they are thirsty, give them something to drink; for by doing this you will heap burning coals on their heads." Do not be overcome by evil, but overcome evil with good.

In Rom 13:1–10, Paul deals with the governing authorities. His concern is how to show love toward people in society. He expects Christians to honor the authorities and pay taxes. Otherwise, his point is not that Christians should blindly obey even the evil power but that they must do their best in loving people because "love does no wrong to a neighbor; therefore, love is the fulfilling of the law" (Rom 13:10). His advice to his readers continues in Rom 14–15, in which he asks them to welcome the weak and to take care of them (Rom 14:1–23; 15:7).

"New Life" in Galatians

In Galatians, Paul's theology of good news / gospel includes new life in Christ. New life begins with faith that participates in Christ. This argument is made in Gal 2:16–21. One can be set right with God through Christ's faithfulness. The new life begins not with the law but with faith. Even before faith, there must be God's promise and grace. Abraham exemplifies new life in hope of God's promise. Though he was old and poor, he received God's promise and blessing. He had a sense of responsibility for this blessing. He trusted God and walked with him in faith to the end in anticipation of God's promised new future. Paul argues that Christ came to be that new future, to fulfill the promise of God, which was given to Abraham. Thus the gentiles who come to faith through Christ will be blessed and become children of God.

But in the churches of Galatia, some people preached a different kind of gospel. They taught that in addition to faith, membership in God's people requires that gentiles observe circumcision and other particular Jewish laws. But Paul reminds the Galatians that "the only thing that counts is faith working through love." That is, "In Christ Jesus neither circumcision nor uncircumcision counts for anything" (Gal 5:6). When one participates in Christ's faithfulness—that is, when one is in Christ—they should live faithfully as Christ did. Such faith will bear the fruit of love. Where there is proper faith following Christ's examples of life, the law may be kept as long as it helps one live faithfully and love neighbors (Gal 5:6, 14).

To maintain the new life in Christ, therefore, one should not turn back to the old habits of honoring the elemental spirits (Gal 4:8–11). The Galatians must come back to the heart of the gospel of Christ (Gal 4:12–20). They must know the advantage of the gospel: to become children of God. They are the promised people of God. As people of God, they have to maintain this advantage of the gospel by standing firm in Christ. They should not submit again to the yoke of slavery (Gal 5:1–15). They have to live by the Spirit (Gal 5:16–26) and fulfill the law of Christ (Gal 6:1–10).

"New Life" in 1 Corinthians

In the Corinthian correspondence, we learn that new life in Christ needs to be built on Christ: his faithfulness, his love, and his grace. Christ exemplified God's love and his righteousness through faithfulness. Thus the foundation of the church is Christ (1 Cor 3:11). All who follow Jesus must be united to him, having the same mind and purpose (1 Cor 1:10; 6:12–20). Being united to him means to follow Christ and live by his faith (cf. Gal 2:20). New life requires separation from all forms of evil acts or evil thinking. The purpose of new life is to glorify God, which demands Christlike devotion to embodying God's love, peace, and justice in the world.

New life in Christ also means a new way of community, as Paul says in 1 Cor 12:12–27. The new community of love is not a mere gathering of Christians who confess that Jesus is the Lord but a radical community of love in which members live according to Christ. The body of Christ metaphor in 1 Cor 12 implies a double meaning: both a way of living and a Christlike community. "The body of Christ" may be read as a *Christic body* in the sense that members should live like Christ, imitating his faithful life.[6] Paul's point is not that "you are one unified community in Christ but that you are to live like Christ to form a true community of love." In the next chapter, we will see more about "the body of Christ" in 1 Corinthians and elsewhere.

Paul explains new life in 1 Cor 13. Speaking in the first person, he argues that love is the heart of new life in the community. Love is the most excellent gift and the key ingredient in community. In 1 Cor 13:4–7, Paul describes love as a verb: "Love is patient; love is kind; love is not envious or boastful or arrogant or rude. It does not insist on its own way; it is not irritable or resentful; it does not rejoice in wrongdoing, but rejoices in the truth. It bears all things, believes all things, hopes all things, endures all things." Here, love is not a state of emotion but an action that one either does or does not do: "to be patient" (*makrothymeo*), "to act kindly" (*chresteuomai*), "not to be jealous" (*zeloo*), "not to brag" (*perpereuomai*), "not to be proud" (*physiomai*), "not to behave indecently" (*aschemoneo*), "not to desire" (*zeteo*), "not to be upset" (*paroxynomai*),

---

6. Kim, *Christ's Body in Corinth*, 11–96. See also Kim, "Reclaiming Christ's Body," 20–29.

"not to think of evil" (*logizomai*), "not to rejoice in the wrong-doing" (*chairo*), "to rejoice in the truth" (*synkairo*), "to bear all things" (*stego*), "to believe all things" (*pisteuo*), "to hope all things" (*elpizo*), and "to endure all things" (*hypomeno*).[7] Such love is based not on emotion but on Christ. Thus it never ends. To abide by love, one should give up childish ways (1 Cor 13:11). On the day of the Lord, love will complete faith and hope (1 Cor 13:13).[8] So Paul says, "For now we see in a mirror, dimly, but then we will see face to face. Now I know only in part; then I will know fully, even as I have been fully known" (1 Cor 13:12).

"New Creation" in 2 Cor 5:17–21, Rom 8:21–22, and Gal 6:15

2 Cor 5:17–21

So if anyone is in Christ, there is a new creation: everything old has passed away; see, everything has become new! All this is from God, who reconciled us to himself through Christ and has given us the ministry of reconciliation; that is, in Christ, God was reconciling the world to himself, not counting their trespasses against them, and entrusting the message of reconciliation to us. So we are ambassadors for Christ, since God is making his appeal through us; we entreat you on behalf of Christ, be reconciled to God. For our sake, he made him to be sin who knew no sin so that in him, we might become the righteousness of God.

Rom 8:20–23

For the creation was subjected to futility, not of its own will but by the will of the one who subjected it, in hope that the creation itself will be set free from its bondage to decay and will

---

7. Yung Suk Kim, "Commentary on 1 Cor 13:1–13," *Working Preacher*, accessed January 17, 2020, https://tinyurl.com/yyzgk872.

8. When the Corinthians asked about the future resurrection status on the last day, Paul's answer is bodily transformation, in that there will be "a spiritual body" (1 Cor 15:53–54). In fact, Paul's answer is oxymoronic from the Greek philosophy of dualism between the body and the soul. In this view, the body is rotten and only the soul is immortal. But Paul combines these two impossibles and says there will be a body that is spiritual. His point is that the resurrection of the dead is possible because of God's power.

obtain the freedom of the glory of the children of God. We know that the whole creation has been groaning in labor pains until now; and not only the creation, but we ourselves, who have the first fruits of the Spirit, groan inwardly while we wait for adoption, the redemption of our bodies.

Gal 6:15

For neither circumcision nor uncircumcision is anything; but a new creation is everything!

For Paul, new life and new creation are closely related. New life is the result of one's faithful response to God through Jesus. In it, one is set right with God. New life is justification or reconciliation with God. One lives as a new creation. One does not live by sin but lives by faith. We can read 2 Cor 5:17–19 according to this definition of new life: "So if anyone is in Christ, there is a new creation: everything old has passed away; see, everything has become new! All this is from God, who reconciled us to himself through Christ, and has given us the ministry of reconciliation; that is, in Christ God was reconciling the world to himself, not counting their trespasses against them, and entrusting the message of reconciliation to us." As the new creation is "in Christ" (2 Cor 5:17a), so also in new life "everything old has passed away; see, everything has become new!" (2 Cor 5:17b). All this newness comes from God, who is "the source of your life in Christ Jesus, who became for us wisdom from God, and righteousness and sanctification and redemption" (1 Cor 1:30). Christ is the way that God established for our reconciliation. And now God has given the ministry of reconciliation to his Christ's followers, which means they, as ambassadors of Christ, have to manifest God's righteousness/love through Christ to the world (2 Cor 5:20–21). In that way, they may spread the good news of new life or new creation.

The idea of new creation is also seen in Rom 8:21–23 (cf. 2 Cor 5:2–4). Here, new creation is God renewing creation from decay. This recovery will happen in the future, at the Parousia. Paul envisions the renewal of the whole of creation but argues that the new creation has already begun because of Christ.[9] In the old creation, sin exercised dominion over people who followed their passions. But now with Christ who died to sin and lived to God, one cannot let sin exercise dominion over one's body. This means one has to "put to death the deeds of the body by the Spirit" (Rom 8:13). Then one's new life will continue and will be completed on the day of the Parousia.

Paul's notion of a new creation in Gal 6:15 must be understood in the context of the Galatian heresy. The phrase is a counterargument to those who taught the way of circumcision in the churches of Galatia. In Gal 6, Paul gives final exhortations to the Galatians to fulfill the law of Christ, to bear one another's burdens, and to keep working by the Spirit. They are to fulfill the law of Christ by seeking the way of Christ. As Christ lived for God and loved the world, so too must they. The law of Christ is his faithfulness. So "to fulfill the law of Christ" means to live by his faith and to proclaim the good news that he brought to us: that one is reconciled to God through Jesus, that gentiles can become children of God through faith, and that one is set right with God through Jesus Christ's faithfulness (Gal 2:16). But as Christ's faithfulness is ongoing, so too is Christians' faith in and commitment to God. It is the beginning of a new life. That is why Paul proclaims only Christ crucified (Gal 6:14, 17; 1 Cor 2:2). Christ, who is the foundation of the church (1 Cor 3:11), embodies God's love through his life. His followers must be "ambassadors for Christ" (2 Cor 5:20) because they are "a letter of Christ" (2 Cor 3:3). For Paul, Christ is everything, and anyone who stays in Christ and lives by his faithfulness is a new creation. As he says in Gal 6:15, "For neither circumcision nor uncircumcision is anything; but a new creation is everything!" and, earlier in the letter, "It is no longer I who live, but it is Christ who lives in me. And the life I now live in the flesh I live *by the faith of the Son of God,* who loved me and gave himself for me" (italics indicate my translation).

9. Leander Keck, *Romans* (Nashville: Abingdon, 2005), 210.

New creation is by God and comes through Jesus. It is effective for those who live by Christ's faithfulness. Those who participate in Christ must follow the way of Christ: his love and faith.

SUMMARY

New life in Christ must be realistic, experiential, holistic, and apocalyptic. It is not otherworldly or simply existential. New life in Christ is experienced in the here and now. Though "complete" new life is yet to come, one can live a completely new life in God through Christ. One has a new identity in God and finds peace and justice with God. For Paul, new life is synonymous with new creation. The old style of life has passed, and a new one has taken its place. One may find peace within the self because one accepts one's weakness and depends on God. One feels honor and grace because of the Lord Jesus who loved and gave himself for the world. One feels love and responsibility for the world, which is not the enemy but the place to fill with love and grace. One does not seek the wisdom of the world but depends on the wisdom of God that comes through Jesus. One endures hardships and trusts God and Christ in any circumstance because nothing will separate one in Christ from the love of God. The assurance that one belongs to God makes one feel great yet humble. As we have seen earlier, new life is experienced in the here and now. It is holistic, covering both personal and communal matters. It is apocalyptic in the sense that we are not in control of time. The job of the Christian is to follow Christ and live a new life empowered by the Holy Spirit.

New life differs from the "once and for all justification." The latter emphasizes one's complete, onetime legal status that guarantees salvation in the hereafter. God is a judge who declares a verdict of innocence because of Jesus's vicarious death. This is the forensic concept of salvation. But Paul does not talk about salvation this way in his undisputed letters. For the Paul of the undisputed letters, the purpose of Jesus's death is not forensic; rather, it is the result of his obedience to God. He demonstrated God's righteousness, and the political and religious leaders were opposed to that righteousness. Jesus was faithful to God's mission, and because of that, he was crucified. In other words, Paul locates Christ's love and grace in his life and death. This sacrificial, exemplary life is the basis of faith for his followers. Thus human participation is necessary. As Paul says in Rom 3:26, "God justifies the one who has the faith of Jesus" (my translation). In sum, new life is not born once and for all. It is a metaphor according to which one has a new relationship with God. It is possible through Christ and human participation in him. For the Christian, following Jesus is new life, and by living this new life, one grows in sanctification.

New life begins with a new relationship with God when one responds to God's grace. But it is maintained through ongoing commitment to God. As we saw, in Rom 6–8, Paul talks about the maintenance of new life in terms of dying to sin and dying to the law. "Dying to sin" means overcoming sin's temptation or putting to death the sinful passions. Christ also died to sin and lived to God. "Dying to the law" means not to prioritize anything above faith. The law may be kept with informed faith, but it is subsequent to faith and relativized by it.

New life has purposes beyond mere enjoyment. Some Corinthians thought they were free to do anything once they were saved. But Paul contends that their salvation is not done yet and that they have to work it out. The purpose of new life is to edify the community in Christ and spread the good news of Jesus Christ to all. Likewise, new life means engaging the world. One has to see the pain and suffering of others and bring the good news to them so that they may find comfort, peace, and love from God.

QUESTIONS FOR REFLECTION

1. Usually, "new life" in Paul's letters is understood as "life" that is born once and for all. Likewise, one's justification is understood as a status of once and for all, as in the forensic

salvation. Similarly, some consider the birth language used by Jesus in John 3:3 as some sense of literal birth: "No one can see the kingdom of God unless they are born *again* [*anothen*]" (NIV; italics mine). But since the Greek adverb *anothen* has a double meaning—"again" or "from above"—we have to wonder which sense Jesus means. He seems to say one must be born from above, which means one should be led by God or the Spirit. In other words, birth is used as a metaphor that represents a new relationship with God. Paul's thinking is close to Jesus's. What do you think about this conclusion?

2. In today's world, what are the most important aspects of new life that we need? What are personal needs for a new life? What are communal needs for new life?

3. What would be your theological or practical advice to maintain a new life?

8

THE BODY OF CHRIST

OVERVIEW

Paul uses the phrase "the body of Christ" often in 1–2 Corinthians, Galatians, and Romans. For example, in 1 Cor 6:12–20, he talks about Christ as the body and the Corinthian Christians as the "parts" (*melē*) of Christ (1 Cor 6:15). The Greek noun *melos* (*melē* in the plural) means both "part/member" in the body (like a hand or leg) and "member" of an organism in a community. So "parts of Christ" may refer to the members of the Corinthian community, but it also can mean "parts of Christ's body" in a literal body sense. Paul seems to use the term in this latter sense when he talks about Christ and a prostitute. He juxtaposes "parts/members of Christ" with "parts/members of a prostitute" in 1 Cor 6:15–16: "Do you not know that your bodies are members of Christ? Should I therefore take the members of Christ and make them members of a prostitute? Never! Do you not know that whoever is united to a prostitute becomes one body with her?" Here, Paul talks about the human body, not a metaphorical organism. Furthermore, he says, "Your *bodies* are members of Christ" (italics mine). Paul's concern is that some Corinthians do not care about their bodies and are involved in sexual immorality. He reminds them that they are united to Christ, which means they should use their bodies carefully and honorably. For Christians, body and spirit cannot be separated from each other, because, as Paul says, "anyone united to the Lord becomes one spirit with him" (1 Cor 6:17). Their bodies are a temple of the Spirit, and thus they must glorify God in their bodies (1 Cor 6:20). Paul's use of "body of Christ" implies more than an organism, more than mere belonging to the church of Christ. Rather, his primary concern is ethical in that the Corinthian members need to live *in their bodies* according to Christ's spirit and his work.

Similarly, in 1 Cor 12:27, Paul talks about the importance of the Corinthians living in Christ: "Now you are the body of Christ and individually members of it." Traditionally, "the body of Christ" has been understood as a metaphorical organism: "You are the community belonging to Christ and you are individually members of it."[1] But does Paul really mean this sense of an organism? An alternative interpretation considers the body phrase as a metaphor for "a way of living," as we saw in 1 Cor 6:12–20. According to this interpretation, the body of Christ is Christic life or Christic community.[2] As we will see later, the point is that members of the community (church) should be informed by Christ and live like him, both individually and communally. This interpretation makes more sense than the traditional one because, for Paul, the body of Christ is not limited to the community or the church. The church/community is built on Christ, and Christ is the foundation of the church. Thus, in the undisputed letters, "the body of Christ" is not synonymous with the church (*ekklesia*). There, Paul usually refers to "the church of God" (1 Cor 1:2; 10:32; 11:32; 15:9; 2 Cor 1:1; Gal 1:13). Only in the Deutero-Pauline letters do we see the merging of "the body of Christ" with the church (Col 1:18, 24; Eph 5:23). It would be very difficult, then, to talk about Paul's gospel without talking about the body of Christ that was broken and crucified for God's righteousness.

---

1. Margaret Mitchell, *Paul and the Rhetoric of Reconciliation: An Exegetical Investigation of the Language and Composition of 1 Corinthians* (Louisville: Westminster John Knox, 1987), 20–64. See also Jerome Neyrey, *Paul in Other Words: A Cultural Reading of His Letter* (Louisville: Westminster John Knox, 1990), 115.

2. Kim, *Christ's Body in Corinth*, 65–96.

Paul hints at this idea of Christ's sacrifice in 2 Cor 13:4: "For he was crucified *by weakness* [*ex astheneias*], but lives by the power of God. For we are weak in him, but in dealing with you we will live with him by the power of God" (italics indicate my translation). Jesus could have avoided crucifixion if he had stopped teaching the good news of the kingdom of God. But he was willing to die for God's righteousness, and so he did not cease to teach. He was crucified by weakness (*ex astheneias*), which implies his death is tragic.

Paul's body politic is distinguished from that of the Stoics of his time. They promote a rigidly hierarchical vision of society in which all people were unified by virtue of their place in the hierarchy. In the ancient patron-client system, survival often means giving service to a benefactor. Protesting against the system incurs severe punishment. But Paul's view of community is different. All members of the church are respected and share suffering together like the real body. In the Stoic worldview, suffering is not properly dealt with and is considered the price paid for the sake of a stable society. Paul's point is not that the church is one unified community in itself but rather that it is a union with Christ. When talking about Paul's view of community, union—not unity—is preferable language. The foundation of this union is Christ, who gave himself for the members of the church. In this union, members of the church must live in accordance with Christ's example. When they do so, they are united to Christ and can help one another, sharing one another's pain and rejoicing one another's joys.

GRECO-ROMAN AND JEWISH TEXTS AND CONTEXTS

Imperial Roman society is a hegemonic and hierarchical body politic. The emperor is on top of the social rank, and slaves are at the bottom. The elites are rich and honored. They are society's leaders, and others have to submit to them. Slaves are without honor or status. No complaints or protests against the system are allowed. The fundamental truth of the social order is the concord or unity that all members of society must support. As the Roman historian Livy notes of the famous Menenius Agrippa fable,

> In the days when man's members did not all agree amongst themselves, as is now the case, but had each its own ideas and a voice of its own, the other parts thought it unfair that they should have the worry and the trouble and the labour of providing everything for the belly, while the belly remained quietly in their midst with nothing to do but to enjoy the good things which they bestowed upon it; they therefore conspired together that the hands should carry no food to the mouth, nor the mouth accept anything that was given it, nor the teeth grind up what they received. While they sought in this angry spirit to starve the belly into submission, the members themselves and the whole body were reduced to the utmost weakness. Hence it had become clear that even the belly had no idle task to perform, and was no more nourished than it nourished the rest, by giving out to all parts of the body that by which we live and thrive, when it has been divided equally amongst the veins and is enriched with digested food—that is, the blood. Drawing a parallel from this to show how like was the internal dissension of the bodily members to the anger of the plebs against the Fathers, he prevailed upon the minds of his hearers.[3]

The hegemonic body politic is based on ancient Greek political philosophy and is a common subject throughout Greco-Roman literature.[4] In the *Timaeus*, Plato conceives of the whole cosmos as one hierarchical body structured by four kinds of living bodies and the four elements of the physical world.[5] This hierarchy is as large as the cosmos and as intimate as the human soul. As we saw in a previous chapter, Plato divides the soul into three parts: the reasonable (*logistikon*), the

---

3. Livy, *History of Rome*, 2.32.9–12.

4. For more, see Daniel Smith, "Why Paul's Fabulous Body Is Missing Its Belly: The Rhetorical Subversion of Menenius Agrippa's Fable in 1 Corinthians 12.12–30," *Journal for the Study of the New Testament* 41, no. 2 (2018): 143–60.

5. Plato, *Timaeus*, Perseus Digital Library, accessed September 28, 2020, 40A, https://tinyurl.com/yxbfmrhc.

courageous (*thumoeides*), the appetitive (*epithumetikon*).[6] The reasonable part is eternal, and those who have more of this part must rule society.[7] Likewise, he sees the human body hierarchically. The head is the most divine part of the body, ruling the rest of it.[8] It represents the male.[9] Barbarians and slaves are less human.[10]

Aristotle's worldview echoes Plato's. He also thinks the mind (*nous*) is divine. Male is superior to female because a woman is "a deformed male."[11] He also says that man is "hot, fertile, perfectly formed and contributes soul to the generation of a new being; woman is cold, infertile, deformed and contributes the body."[12]

Stoicism further develops the hegemonic body politic and supports the dominant ideology of concord/unity in the Roman Empire. Manilius talks about the hierarchical universe run by the divine spirit: "This fabric which forms the body of the boundless universe, together with its members composed of nature's diverse elements, air and fire, earth and level sea, is ruled by the force of a divine spirit; by sacred dispensation the deity brings harmony and governs with hidden purpose, arranging mutual bonds between all parts, so that . . . the whole may stand fast in kinship despite its variety of forms."[13] As a corollary, Stoics argue the wise should rule the foolish because the wise have *logos*.[14] In their rationality,

6. Plato, *Republic*, Perseus Digital Library, accessed September 28, 2020, 439C–441B, https://tinyurl.com/h5alxu4.

7. Plato, 370A–B.

8. Plato, *Timaeus*, 44D; 90A, B.

9. Plato, 42B; Plato, *Laws*, Perseus Digital Library, accessed September 28, 2020, 781A, https://tinyurl.com/y2opnou8.

10. Plato, *Republic*, 469B–471C.

11. Aristotle, *On the Generation of Animals*, UNSW Embryology, accessed September 28, 2020, IV 3 767a36–b15, https://tinyurl.com/y5eces6p.

12. Ioan P. Culianu, "Introduction: The Body Reexamined," in *Religious Reflections on the Human Body*, ed. Jane Marie Law (Bloomington: Indiana University Press, 1995), 1–18.

13. Manilius, *Astronomica*, trans. G. P. Goold (Cambridge, MA: Harvard University Press, 1977), 1.247–54.

14. Seneca, *De beneficiis*, Stoics, accessed September 28, 2020, 1.10.3–4; 4.27.1–3, https://tinyurl.com/yxr2d5st.

they never challenge society's status quo but instead empha-size the ideal of complete societal unity.

In first-century CE Palestine, Jewish elites like the Saddu-cees affirm the hegemonic body politic because their power is based on collaboration with Rome. The Pharisees do not share the status or power of the Sadducees, and they advo-cate for reforms popular among the Jewish people. They draw their power and influence from the people, and they focus their reforms on the renewal of the law to establish commu-nity on the basis of the law. As a result, community boundaries are important, and those who do not keep the law such as sin-ners, tax collectors, and prostitutes do not belong to the com-munity. The Zealots oppose the Roman hegemony directly through armed revolt and their quest for the Jewish state, while the Essenes form their own sectarian, ascetic commu-nity that excludes those who do not subscribe to their view.

As a diasporic Jew, Paul was familiar with Stoicism and knew the political situation in Palestine. Even though he does not explicitly mention Stoicism in his undisputed letters, he talks about a body politic that is opposed to the hegemonic body politic. In the next section, we will analyze his discus-sion of the body politics in the Corinthian correspondence and Romans, among other texts.

"THE BODY OF CHRIST" IN PAUL'S LETTERS

In Paul's theology, the concept of the body is used in var-ious ways. First, body means the whole life of a person, as we see in 1 Cor 6:12–20. It is a neutral term that may be used positively or negatively, depending on the person's attitude. He does not believe that the body is intrinsically evil, and he rejects the dualism between the body and the spirit. The body is the place in which the Holy Spirit dwells, and because of this, Christians are to glorify God in and with their bodies. To glorify God, they have to put to death their sinful passions. Second, Paul talks about Christ's body or Christ crucified. His body was broken, and he was crucified by weakness. Paul draws out the significance of this event for Christ's followers.

Third, Paul considers "the body of Christ" and its relation to his followers. For example, 1 Cor 12:27 reads, "You are the body of Christ and individually members of it." Fourth, Paul speaks of the body of Christ as the eucharistic body.

The Body of Christ as Christ Crucified

Paul says to the chaotic church in Corinth that he decided to proclaim only Christ crucified (1 Cor 1:23; 2:2). Some Corinthians did not care for the weak and marginalized, seeking their own power and glory. They forgot why Christ was crucified. Paul reminds them of the message about the cross, which reveals the power of God through which many powerless people came to join God's household. Christ's crucifixion is the result of his demonstration of God's power and wisdom. He was crucified for his challenge to the wisdom of the world (1 Cor 1:18–25). Through Christ's sacrifice and his love for the weak and despised, "God chose what is foolish in the world to shame the wise; God chose what is weak in the world to shame the strong; God chose what is low and despised in the world, things that are not, to reduce to nothing things that are" (1 Cor 1:27–28). In this sense, Christ represents the power of God, which seems weak but is stronger than human strength. He also represents the wisdom of God, which seems foolish but is wiser than human wisdom (1 Cor 1:25).

In 1 Cor 2:1–5, Paul reminds them of what he proclaimed to the Corinthians: "When I came to you, brothers and sisters, I did not come proclaiming the mystery of God to you in lofty words or wisdom. For I decided to know nothing among you except Jesus Christ, and him crucified. And I came to you in weakness and in fear and in much trembling. My speech and my proclamation were not with plausible words of wisdom, but with a demonstration of the Spirit and of power, so that your faith might rest not on human wisdom but on the power of God." Here, Paul makes clear that the focus of his message is Christ crucified, not Christ resurrected.[15] The power of God

---

15. See Love Sechrest, "Identity and Embodiment of Privilege in Corinth," in *1–2 Corinthians*, ed. Yung Suk Kim (Minneapolis: Fortress, 2013), 9–30. She argues that true Christian privilege and identity must be rooted in the way Christ lived.

affects the resurrection of Christ. God made Christ live by his power (2 Cor 13:4). Christ is not the cause of his own resurrection. But Christ's crucifixion happened because he was doing the work of God. This implies that the Corinthians also need to follow the spirit of Jesus, who risked his life and died for loving the weak and the marginalized. In Galatians, Paul tells his readers that he has been crucified with Christ through faith and that Christ and Christ's faith is the reason he now lives (Gal 2:19–20). Paul carries the crucifixion image even further in Gal 6:17, where he writes, "From now on, let no one make trouble for me; for I carry the marks of Jesus branded on my body." Similar language appears in Philippians 3:8: "I regard everything as loss because of the surpassing value of knowing Christ Jesus my Lord. For his sake I have suffered the loss of all things, and I regard them as rubbish, in order that I may gain Christ" (see also 1 Cor 4:13). Paul's message about the cross is manifold: God's love, Jesus's love, God's justice, and God's judgment.

First, God's love is confirmed on the cross through his Son, who did not spare his own life in demonstrating God's righteousness and proclaiming God's good news. As Paul says in Rom 5:8, "But God proves his love for us in that while we still were sinners Christ died for us." God did not require his Son to be crucified on the cross for human salvation. It is not the violence of the cross but rather Christ's voluntary spirit of self-sacrifice that reveals God's love.

Second, the cross reveals Jesus's love for both God and the world in that he sacrificed himself willingly in order to make manifest God's love for the poor and marginalized. For this reason, Paul writes in 2 Cor 5:14–15, "For the love of Christ urges us on, because we are convinced that one has died for all; therefore all have died. And he died for all, so that those who live might live no longer for themselves, but for him who died and was raised for them." In Rom 8:34–35, Paul again affirms the love of Christ: "Who is to condemn? It is Christ Jesus, who died, yes, who was raised, who is at the right hand of God, who indeed intercedes for us. Who will separate us from the love of Christ? Will hardship, or distress, or persecution, or famine, or nakedness, or peril, or sword?" Paul thus not only distinguishes between but also interrelates the love of God and the love of Jesus. The interrelationship between these loves motivates him to write the famous words of Rom 8:38–39: "For I am convinced that neither death, nor life, nor angels, nor rulers, nor things present, nor things to come, nor powers, nor height, nor depth, nor anything else in all creation, will be able to separate us from the love of God in Christ Jesus our Lord."

Third, the cross reveals God's justice. While propitiatory atonement models suggest that Christ's suffering and death are what "satisfies" God's wrathful, retributive demand for justice, Paul's theology of the cross is much different. The torture and execution of Jesus were acts of injustice and evil. Thus, for Paul, the crucifixion is neither a demand of divine justice nor an indication of divine failure. Rather, God's justice is manifested in vindicating the Son from death itself. Paul makes clear that God's power made his Son live (2 Cor 13:4). God vindicated Jesus and glorified him.

Finally, the cross demonstrates God's judgment. Those who are evil are held accountable for their work. God will destroy the wisdom of the wise and the wisdom of the world (1 Cor 1:18–20).

The Body of Christ as the Christic Life and Christic Community

"The body of Christ" in 1 Cor 12:12–27 and Rom 12:4–5 has been traditionally understood as a metaphorical organism with a focus on concord (unity) in a manner consistent with Stoic political philosophy. But this interpretation needs to be challenged. An alternative understanding reads the body language as a metaphor for a way of living. That is, Christ is an adjectival modifier to the body: Christlike or Christic in the sense of a Christlike way of life. This way of using the Greek genitive case is found in Rom 6:6: "the body of sin" as "the sinful body."[16] So one can translate 1 Cor 12:27 in this way: "You are the Christic body and individually constitute it." This idea

---

16. Kim, *Christ's Body in Corinth*, 11–96. See also Kim, "Reclaiming Christ's Body," 20–29.

of Christ's relation to the body is also seen in 1 Cor 6:17: "But anyone united to the Lord becomes one spirit with him."

If the body metaphor is interpreted in this manner, we can understand "the body of Christ" in two related ways. One is focused on the individual embodiment of Christ in one's life: "Christlike living" or "Christic life." Each Christian should follow Christ and his faithfulness, spreading the good news of Christ and edifying the beloved community as an outworking of individual responsibility for the gospel of Christ. The other aspect of a Christlike living focuses on the community: a Christic community. Paul explains such community in 1 Cor 12:12–27. All parts/members of the body (community) are united to Christ. Their union means they rejoice and suffer together. Rom 12:4–5 also can be understood this way: "For as in one body we have many members, and not all the members have the same function, so we, who are many, are one body in Christ, and individually we are members one of another." Here "one body in Christ" means all are united to him. Therefore, they have to take care of each other. In the body, all parts are taken care of, and their relationship is complementary. Hippocrates points out the importance of union in the body:[17]

> 1.1 In my view, there is no beginning in the body; but everything is alike beginning and end. For when a circle has been drawn, its beginning is not to be found.

> 1.4 The body is homogenous (lit. the same as itself) and is composed of the same things, though not in uniform disposition, in its small parts and its large; in parts above and parts below. And if you like to take the smallest part of the body and injure it, the whole body will feel the injury, whatever sort it may be, for this reason, that the smallest part of the body has all the things that the biggest part has.

> 1.5 This smallest part refers to its own entity whatever it may experience, whether it be bad or good. And for this reason the

---

17. Hippocrates, *Places in Man*, trans. Elizabeth Craik (Oxford: Clarendon, 1998), 37–39.

body feels pain or pleasure from its smallest constituent because all parts exist in the smallest part and these refer everything to each of their own related parts, and register everything.

Hippocrates's idea of union in the body is close to Paul's view of the body, which is an organism of solidarity. So pain in the body is taken seriously and shared by all members of its union.

This alternative interpretation of the body is very different from the Stoic ideal of unity shared with the traditional interpretation of Paul. For the latter, suffering is taken for granted and receives no relief. The better interpretation of the body language in 1 Cor 12:12–27 is the community of union with Christ. The point is not that the community is simply one or unified but that it is in union with Christ, who is the foundation of the church. Christ's followers must be united with the same mind and purpose of Jesus, which means following him in his faithfulness (1 Cor 1:10).

For Paul, the community must be informed by Christ and led by the Spirit. It is the Christic community to which all are welcomed, and all are united to him in and by his faithfulness (1 Cor 12:13; cf. Gal 3:28). All members are respected and allowed to exercise their unique functions and gifts as part of the whole. The goal of the community is to spread the gospel of Christ, which is about faith, hope, and love.

The Body of Christ as the Eucharistic Body

Paul uses the body of Christ in his discussion of the Lord's Supper (1 Cor 11:23–26). Echoing Jesus's own words of institution, he writes, "This is my body that is for you. Do this in remembrance of me" (1 Cor 11:24). At the Lord's Supper, Christ's followers are enjoined to remember his death and celebrate his faithful life. It is a time to embrace Jesus's love and share his love with one another. The Lord's Supper is more than a simple ritual to symbolize the unity of the body's members. It is the union of different members with Christ. For this reason, the members of Christ's body must live lives worthy of this union. Otherwise, the Lord's Supper may be the occasion where some are boastful about their power. Paul goes so far as to warn the Corinthians that their unworthy manner of celebrating the Lord's Supper invites divine judgment.

SUMMARY

Paul conceives of the body holistically. A person is responsible for their own body, and Christians are charged with exercising that responsibility in a way worthy of union with Christ. In Paul's language, they have to glorify God in their bodies.

When Paul speaks of "the body of Christ," we can discern both an individual and a social meaning. Individually, the followers of Jesus are to live like Christ. When Paul says that "you are the body of Christ," he is referring to the Christic life of the individual Christian, who should be informed by Christ and stay in Christ. Individual Christic life also means living by the Spirit and thereby putting to death all sinful passions. Each Christian must live faithfully and spread the gospel of Christ to all. But Paul also intends "the body of Christ" to denote the Christic community as a whole. Individuals are parts/members of the community that is in union with Christ.

Paul's theology of the body also includes Christ's crucified body. The fact that the Son of God was crucified has implications for four central elements of Christian theology: God's love, Jesus's love, God's justice, and God's judgment. For Paul, Christ crucified represents God's power and wisdom that chooses the foolish, the weak, and the despised. Christ showed God's love, God's justice, and God's judgment through his obedience to God's will, even unto death.

Christ crucified is what is remembered in the Lord's Supper. What is celebrated is not Christ's resurrection but his life and death. Paul charges each Christian to evaluate their conduct so as not to disrupt its union with Christ. Lastly, Paul's language focuses on union rather than unity. The latter is the language of the Roman Empire and legitimates hierarchy. But in the union of Christ's community, there is no hierarchy. Christ is not the head of the body, as in Col 1:18 and 1:24. Christ is the body to which all members are united. In the image of union, differences are gathered and maintained as far as members share the core value of a Christ-informed community.

QUESTIONS FOR REFLECTION

1. What is Paul's concept of the human body? How does he relate it to Christ and God?

2. For Paul, "the body of Christ" is too important to refer to the church only. Whenever he refers to the church, he uses "the church of God," not "the church of Christ." He uses the body of Christ in various ways: Christ crucified, Christic life, Christic community, and the eucharistic body. Why do you think it is important to see the diverse uses of the body of Christ?

3. In 1 Cor 6:15, Paul says, "Your bodies are parts/members of Christ." Does he mean the Corinthians are members of the church that belongs to Christ or that they are united to Christ, following his spirit? Is this saying of 1 Cor 6:15 similar to, or different from, 1 Cor 12:27?

4. What is the benefit of reading "the body of Christ" as a union and not a unity?

5. Does the reading of the body of Christ as a metaphor for "a way of living" make sense to you?

6. In the expression "You are the body of Christ," can you read "the body of Christ" as both Christic life and Christic community?

9

THE HOLY SPIRIT

OVERVIEW

This final chapter concerns the identity and role of the Holy Spirit in Paul's undisputed letters. The Greek word *pneuma* means "breath," "wind," or "spirit." We cannot live even a single moment without breath. In Gen 1:2, the wind (*ruach* in Hebrew) from God hovered over the waters at the time of chaos and darkness and participated in God's creation. In Gen 2:7, the Lord made the first human being, Adam, from the dust of the ground and "breathed into his nostrils the breath of life." Humans live by the breath of life that comes from God. But in Paul's letters, the Holy Spirit has further roles to play in the gospel drama.

In the Hebrew Bible, the spirit of God frequently appears.[1] For example, Job 33:4 says, "The spirit of God has made me, and the breath of the Almighty gives me life." The spirit of God is also referred to as a "divine spirit" (Exod 31:3; 35:31), "the spirit of the Lord" (frequently in Judges and 1 Samuel),[2] and "the holy spirit" (Ps 51:11; Isa 63:10–11). In Ps 51:11, the writer pleads with God, "Do not cast me away from your presence,

---

1. Gen 41:38; Num 24:2; 1 Sam 10:10; 11:6; 19:20, 23; 2 Chr 15:1; 24:20; Job 27:3; 33:4; Ezek 11:24.

2. Judg 3:10; 6:34; 11:29; 13:25; 14:6, 19; 15:14; 1 Sam 10:6; 16:13f; 2 Sam 23:2; 1 Kgs 18:12; 22:24; 2 Kgs 2:16; 2 Chr 18:23; 20:14; Isa 11:2; 40:13; 61:1; 63:14; Ezek 11:5; 37:1; Mic 3:8.

and do not take your holy spirit from me." And in Isa 63:10–11, the prophet notes, "But they rebelled and grieved his holy spirit. . . . Where is the one who brought them up out of the sea with the shepherds of his flock? Where is the one who put within them his holy spirit?"

Indeed, the term *spirit* appears more than two hundred times in the Hebrew Bible under a variety of descriptions. For example, there are the spirit of God, an evil spirit, a person's spirit, a spirit of something (jealousy or confusion, for example), and the spirit of wisdom. As a diasporic Jew well educated in Israel's scripture, Paul was familiar with the spirit tradition in the Hebrew Bible.

In the Psalms, the Holy Spirit comforts and guides people in their turmoil. They pray for renewal or restoration. They seek the presence of God. And when they do, they seek the spirit. Thus the psalmist writes, "Do not cast me away from your presence, and do not take your holy spirit from me" (Ps 51:11); "When you send forth your spirit, they are created; and you renew the face of the ground" (Ps 104:30); "Where can I go from your spirit? Or where can I flee from your presence?" (Ps 139:7).

In prophetic literature, the vibrant spirit of God speaks to his agents and sends them on their missions. In Isa 61:1 (quoted in Luke 4:18), the prophet says, "The spirit of the Lord God is upon me, because the Lord has anointed me; he has sent me to bring good news to the oppressed, to bind up the brokenhearted, to proclaim liberty to the captives, and release to the prisoners." The prophet Ezekiel was lifted up and saw a new vision by the spirit of God: "The spirit lifted me up and brought me in a vision by the spirit of God into Chaldea, to the exiles. Then the vision that I had seen left me" (Ezek 11:24).

Paul's undisputed letters are full of "spirit" (*pneuma*) language, which appears more than one hundred times.[3] He uses the term freely, referring to God, Jesus, the Holy Spirit, the human spirit, and the spirit in general. He often talks about

---

3. About the role of the Spirit in Paul's letters, see Gordon Fee, *God's Empowering Presence: The Holy Spirit in the Letters of Paul* (Peabody, MA: Hendrickson, 1994), 839.

the "spirit of God."[4] For example, in Rom 15:19, he writes, "By the power of signs and wonders, by the power of the Spirit of God, so that from Jerusalem and as far around as Illyricum I have fully proclaimed the good news of Christ." Similar language appears in 1 Cor 2:11: "For what human being knows what is truly human except the human spirit that is within? So also no one comprehends what is truly God's except the Spirit of God." Paul also uses the spirit of God in various ways: "the Spirit of our God" (1 Cor 6:11), "the Spirit of the living God" (2 Cor 3:3), or simply "the Spirit."[5] He also uses the Holy Spirit frequently. At other times, he refers to the Spirit of Jesus and relates it to the spirit of God, as Rom 8:9 says, "But you are not in the flesh; you are in the Spirit, since the Spirit of God dwells in you. Anyone who does not have the Spirit of Christ does not belong to him." Similarly, in Gal 4:6 and Phil 1:19, he talks about the Spirit of Jesus. In Gal 4:6, he writes, "And because you are children, God has sent the Spirit of his Son into our hearts, crying, 'Abba! Father!'" And in Phil 1:19, he notes, "For I know that through your prayers and the help of the Spirit of Jesus Christ this will turn out for my deliverance." Paul also writes of "the spirit" in a more general sense: "my spirit" (Rom 1:9; 1 Cor 5:4; 14:14; 16:18), "your spirit" (Gal 6:18; Phlm 1:25), "one spirit" (1 Cor 6:17), and "the spirit of holiness" (Rom 1:4).

For Paul, the Spirit or the Holy Spirit helps God in his work. He refers to "things God has revealed to us through the Spirit" (1 Cor 2:10), to the Spirit that "intercedes for the saints according to the will of God" (Rom 8:27), and to the Holy Spirit that assures God's love for his children (Rom 8:16; Gal 4:6). The Spirit also has to do with Jesus: "Now the Lord is the Spirit, and where the Spirit of the Lord is, there is freedom" (2 Cor 3:17). The Spirit of Jesus does the work of the Holy Spirit. The Spirit gives aid to the followers of Jesus and strengthens them in their faith (1 Cor 12:3).

4. Rom 8:9, 14; 15:19; 1 Cor 2:11; 7:40; 12:3.

5. Rom 1:4; 7:6; 8:2, 4–6, 9–11, 13, 6, 23, 26–27; 15:30; 1 Cor 2:4, 10, 12–13; 12:4, 7–9, 11, 13; 14:2; 2 Cor 3:6, 8, 17; 5:5; Gal 3:2–3, 5, 14; 4:29; 5:5, 16–18, 22, 25; 6:1, 8; Phil 2:1; 1 Thess 5:19.

Paul's language of the Holy Spirit is summarized in his benediction formula: "The grace of the Lord Jesus Christ, the love of God, and the communion of the Holy Spirit be with all of you" (2 Cor 13:13). All works of God and of Jesus are possible through the Holy Spirit and for the benefit of God's children.

GRECO-ROMAN AND JEWISH TEXTS AND CONTEXTS

In Stoic philosophy, *pneuma* is understood as the breath of life that constitutes the cosmos, including humans. The highest form of the pneuma is the soul of Zeus, similar to the divine reason or logos. The cosmos is a unified and structured hierarchy with different degrees of pneuma allotted to different degrees of being. Happiness follows upon recognizing one's degree of the pneuma and living without complaint in one's correlated place in society. Stoics emphasize the virtue of self-control and the acceptance of this natural hierarchy. In their worldview, there is no space to talk about the spirit's positive role to help people overcome their privations and limitations. Each person has to cope with their place in the cosmos alone by cultivating the intellectual virtues of wisdom and the moral virtues of prudence, justice, fortitude, and temperance. Stoicism has no liberative solutions to the pain and suffering of the marginalized because the Stoics have no interest in changing the political and moral order. They only offer methods for enduring hardships, not for overcoming them. Because neither the prevailing political order nor its favored philosophies provide the help necessary for improving their lives, many ancient people turn to mystery religions where they are comforted and empowered to live in the midst of all forms of injustices. Many foreign gods and mystery cults were imported to the Roman world and thrived there. Through rituals and gatherings, oppressed people found comfort and assurance of their life in the world.

In Jewish apocalyptic literature, the Holy Spirit enlightens and empowers people to live confidently in difficult times. They are told that "the spirit of the Lord has filled the world, and that which holds all things together knows what is said" (Wis 1:7). The people depend on the Holy Spirit sent from above to give them wisdom (Wis 9:17). The author of 4 Esdras says, "If then I have found favor with you, send the holy spirit into me, and I will write everything that has happened in the world from the beginning, the things that were written in your law, so that people may be able to find the path, and that those who want to live in the last days may do so" (2 Esd 14:22).

In the Hellenistic Jewish context, Philo of Alexandria writes, "And Moses shows us this, when speaking of the creator and maker of the holy work of the creation, in these words: 'And God summoned Bezaleel, and filled him with his Holy Spirit, and with wisdom, and understanding, and knowledge, to be able to devise every work' {Exod 31:1}. So that, what the spirit of God is, is very definitively described in these words."[6] Philo asserts that the spirit of God is everywhere and with his prophets. His notion of the spirit is so all-encompassing that it must be quoted at length:

God, since His fullness is everywhere, is near us, and since His eye beholds us, since He is close beside us, let us refrain from evil-doing. It was best that our motive should be reverence, but if not, let us at least tremble to think of the power of His sovereignty, how invincible it is, how terrible and inexorable in vengeance, when He is minded to use His power of chastisement. Thus may the divine spirit of wisdom not lightly shift His dwelling and be gone, but long, long abide with us, since He did thus abide with Moses the wise.[7]

For when Moses was now on the point of being taken away, and was standing at the very starting-place, as it were, that he might fly away and complete his journey to heaven, he was once more inspired and filled with the Holy Spirit, and while still alive, he

6. Philo, *On the Giants*, Early Christian Writings, accessed September 28, 2020, chap. 5, https://tinyurl.com/yy6y9txq.

7. Philo, *On the Giants*, chap. 11, 469.

prophesied admirably what should happen to himself after his death, relating, that is, how he had died when he was not as yet dead, and how he was buried without any one being present so as to know of his tomb [Deuteronomy 34:6 (!)], because in fact he was entombed not by mortal hands, but by immortal powers.[8]

And if, indeed, any one assuming the name and appearance of a prophet [Deuteronomy 13:1], appearing to be inspired and possessed by the Holy Spirit, were to seek to lead the people to the worship of those who are accounted gods in the different cities, it would not be fitting for the people to attend to him being deceived by the name of a prophet. For such an one is an imposter and not a prophet.[9]

But the class of prophets loves to be subject to such influences; for when it is divining, and when the intellect is inspired with divine things, it no longer exists in itself, since it receives the divine spirit within and permits it to dwell with itself; or rather, as he himself has expressed it, as spirit falls upon him; since it does not come slowly over him, but rushes down upon him suddenly.[10]

In Palestine, the Pharisees are more focused on the law than on the holy spirit. In contrast, Jesus depends on the Spirit and sets time aside for spiritual reflection. Through the Spirit, he proclaims the kingdom of God, heals the sick, and acts for justice. Through the Spirit, he is open to God's power and God's wisdom. In this respect, he is close to the classical prophets who are closely connected with God and the Spirit.

"The holy spirit" appears more than thirty times in the Dead Sea Scrolls.[11] In the scrolls, the Spirit of Truth or the Spirit of Righteousness empowers the faithful to abide by the way

8. Philo, *On the Life of Moses*, Early Jewish Writings, accessed September 28, 2020, II, LI, 291, https://tinyurl.com/y6rd8lr2 (brackets in the original).

9. Philo, *The Special Laws*, Early Jewish Writings, accessed September 28, 2020, I, LVIII, 315, https://tinyurl.com/yyd2oew (brackets in the original).

10. Philo, *Questions and Answers on Genesis*, Early Jewish Writings, accessed September 28, 2020, III, 9, https://tinyurl.com/y5mrksfj.

11. For example, see 1QS 3:7; 4:21; 8:16; 9:3 1QS^b 2:24.

of the Torah and not be corrupted by the way of Jerusalem. The holy spirit teaches the members of the sectarian community that they should live in purity and proclaim the correct teachings concerning the law (1QS 9.3).

THE HOLY SPIRIT IN PAUL'S LETTERS

The Holy Spirit is not only merely power but also the person working alongside God, Jesus, and children of God. Paul articulates this idea in 2 Cor 13:13 when he ends the letter, "The grace of the Lord Jesus Christ, the love of God, and the communion of the Holy Spirit be with all of you" (2 Cor 13:13). In a previous chapter, we talked about Paul's threefold gospel: the gospel of God, the gospel of Christ, and the gospel that Jesus's followers have to proclaim. Ultimately, this threefold gospel depends on the Holy Spirit's aid. Paul understands the Holy Spirit in various ways. It is called the Spirit, the spirit of God, and it is connected to the spirit of Jesus. In the following section, we will analyze these various Pauline descriptions more in depth.

The Holy Spirit Confirming God's Love

In Romans, Paul explains his threefold gospel to the Roman Christians. For him, the gospel begins with God and is the power of God for salvation to everyone who has faith. The centerpiece of the gospel is God's righteousness, which is God's love for all people. This righteousness of God has been manifested in his Son Jesus. Christ is, thus, the good news to the world. Those who share the faithfulness of Jesus are justified by God and live a new life in Christ. As children of God, they proclaim this good news of God through Jesus. Throughout their journey of gospel proclamation, they need the guidance of the Spirit.

In Paul's gospel, the Holy Spirit confirms God's love for those who are justified by faith. Even though they have peace with God, they may encounter hardships and suffering due to Christ (Rom 5:1-2). During such times, their hope in God should not fade "because God's love has been poured into our hearts through the Holy Spirit" (Rom 5:5; see also Rom 15:13). The Spirit also confirms that all who come to God through faith are children of God and that they will be led by the Spirit (Rom 8:15). No matter what happens, the Spirit bears witness with their spirit that they are children of God (Rom 8:16). Paul says that "you did not receive a spirit of slavery to fall back into fear, but you have received a spirit of adoption" (Rom 8:15). When they cry, "Abba! Father!" the Spirit confirms that God's love for them is unchangeable. Gal 4:6 also confirms the assurance of God's love for the Galatians through the sending of the Spirit of Jesus, which is the Holy Spirit: "And because you are children, God has sent the Spirit of his Son into our hearts, crying, 'Abba! Father!'"[12] Paul continues to speak of God's unwavering love for his children: "Likewise the Spirit helps us in our weakness; for we do not know how to pray as we ought, but that very Spirit intercedes with sighs too deep for words. And God, who searches the heart, knows what is the mind of the Spirit, because the Spirit intercedes for the saints according to the will of God" (Rom 8:26–27). Because the Spirit confirms God's love in Christ, in the end, Paul says in Rom 8:38–39, "For I am convinced that neither death, nor life, nor angels, nor rulers, nor things present, nor things to come, nor powers, nor height, nor depth, nor anything else in all creation, will be able to separate us from the love of God in Christ Jesus our Lord." God will not give up on his people and gives "the Spirit as a guarantee" (2 Cor 5:5).

The Holy Spirit Supporting the Gospel of God

The Holy Spirit helps people understand and accept God's gospel. Paul preached the message of the gospel "not in word only, but also in power and in the Holy Spirit and with full conviction" (1 Thess 1:5). Despite persecution, the Thessalonians received the word with joy, and they were inspired by the Holy Spirit (1 Thess 1:6). The Spirit helps the listeners of Paul's message hear its content and inspires the content itself. The Spirit also helps Paul as the speaker deliver the good news boldly. Paul tells the Corinthians, "My speech and my proclamation were

12. The Spirit appears throughout Galatians (3:14; 4:6, 29; 5:16–18, 22–23, 25; 6:1, 8), and its function varies depending on the need of the community.

not with plausible words of wisdom, but with a demonstration of the Spirit and of power, so that your faith might rest not on human wisdom but on the power of God" (1 Cor 2:4–5).

Beyond the Spirit's role in the communication of the gospel, Paul argues that God's wisdom and God's power have been revealed through the mediation of the Holy Spirit (1 Cor 2:10). The Spirit searches everything and even the depths of God (1 Cor 2:10). Here, the Spirit is the spirit of God, and yet the Spirit acts separately for the sake of humanity. The spirit of God comprehends "what is truly God's" (1 Cor 2:11). Therefore, we can trust the Spirit that is from God (1 Cor 2:12). Through the Spirit, we may understand the gifts of God: life, peace, and righteousness. Christians are called to proclaim God's good news and God's power, but it is the Spirit who first teaches these things to them (1 Cor 2:13).

To spread the good news of God, Christians need the power of the spirit of God, as Paul says in Rom 15:19: "By the power of signs and wonders, by the power of the Spirit of God, so that from Jerusalem and as far around as Illyricum I have fully proclaimed the good news of Christ." Without the power of the spirit of God, one must rely on one's own strength or knowledge about the truth. Human strength and knowledge are not enough. The followers of Jesus proclaim the good news of God as "a letter of Christ, prepared by us, written not with ink but with the Spirit of the living God, not on tablets of stone but on tablets of human hearts" (2 Cor 3:3).

The Holy Spirit Confirming Christ Jesus

The Holy Spirit helps people confess that Jesus is the Lord. As Paul says in 1 Cor 12:3, "Therefore I want you to understand that no one speaking by the Spirit of God ever says 'Let Jesus be cursed!' and no one can say 'Jesus is Lord' except by the Holy Spirit." The Spirit confirms the work of Jesus and helps people both understand the significance of Christ's work and confess their allegiance to Christ. For Paul, the resurrected Christ is the Lord and the Spirit himself—the Spirit of the Lord. Paul writes, "Where the Spirit of the Lord is, there is freedom" (2 Cor 3:17). Jesus, the last Adam, became "a life-giving spirit" (1 Cor 15:45).

The Holy Spirit Strengthening the Community

The Corinthian community suffered from divisions.[13] Many boasted about their gifts and did not take care of the whole community. Many of them were in rivalry with other members. Some claimed that they were better than others because of their special spiritual gifts. The problem is they did not ask what they could do for the common good or what the Spirit wanted them to do.

In 1 Cor 12:1–11, Paul explains that the purpose of spiritual gifts is to edify the church. First, he tells the Corinthians that the many gifts are all from the same Spirit. The Spirit does not give to all only one kind of gift. The church needs diverse gifts and services: "the utterance of wisdom," "the utterance of knowledge," "faith," "gifts of healing," "the working of miracles," "prophecy," "the discernment of spirits," "various kinds of tongues," and "the interpretation of tongues" (1 Cor 12:8–10). Second, whoever does the work of the Spirit in the church must reflect the work of Jesus (1 Cor 12:5), who is the foundation of the church. His faithful life serving the weak and oppressed should be a constant reminder to all who work in the name of the Lord. Third, whoever does the work of the Spirit must know that God is the one who activates all works, as Paul says in 1 Cor 12:6: "There are varieties of activities, but it is the same God who activates all of them in everyone." The implication is that members have to test their deeds or works, based on God. Fourth, the purpose of the gifts of the Spirit is "for the common good" (1 Cor 12:7). All members of the church should work together to edify the community. They also have to test everything in the community and should not quench the Spirit (cf. 1 Thess 5:19–20).

The Holy Spirit Leading the Followers of Jesus

The followers of Jesus must continue to live by the faithfulness of Jesus and must be led by the Spirit accordingly. This means

13. This section is an abbreviated version of my contribution to Working Preacher: "Commentary on 1 Cor 12:1–11," Working Preacher, accessed September 28, 2020, https://tinyurl.com/yxk7lklf.

that they have to "put to death the deeds of the body by the Spirit" (Rom 8:13). "The deeds of the body" refers to what Paul elsewhere calls the "sinful passions" that do not seek God's will. Then Paul says somewhat surprisingly, "All who are led by the Spirit of God are children of God." In other words, if one is not led by the Spirit, or if one does not put to death one's sinful passions, one is not the child of God. Paul exhorts to the Galatians to "live by the Spirit, I say, and do not gratify the desires of the flesh. For what the flesh desires is opposed to the Spirit, and what the Spirit desires is opposed to the flesh; for these are opposed to each other, to prevent you from doing what you want" (Gal 5:16–17). If they are led by the Spirit, they may discern the purpose of the law, which is to love the neighbor (Gal 5:14, 18, 25–26). If they are led by the Spirit, they may bear fruit of the Spirit: "love, joy, peace, patience, kindness, generosity, faithfulness, gentleness, and self-control" (Gal 5:22–23). Without the Spirit, their fruit will instead be evil deeds (Gal 5:19–21).[14]

In Corinth, the divided factions were irresponsible in exercising their Christian freedom and disrupted the union of Christ. Paul reminds them that "your bodies are parts/members of Christ." They should be united not to a prostitute but to Christ. Union to Christ means they have to live faithfully like Christ. The means of their unity, according to Paul, is the Spirit. When they are in union with Christ, they are "a temple of the Holy Spirit" (1 Cor 6:19).

SUMMARY

Pneuma means breath, wind, or spirit. Human beings live because of the breath given to them by God. But beyond mere respiration, humans need their spirits refreshed by God and his Spirit each day. For Paul, this Spirit is both humanity's beginning (when we were created) and its end (eternal life). In moments of uncertainty, the Spirit testifies to

14. For example, the vice list includes the following: "fornication, impurity, licentiousness, idolatry, sorcery, enmities, strife, jealousy, anger, quarrels, dissensions, factions" (Gal 5:19–20).

God's unchanging love in Christ (Rom 8). The Spirit knows all things and helps Christians in their weaknesses. The Spirit searches everything and even the depths of God (1 Cor 2:10). Christians have assurance because the spirit of God is with them.

In Paul's undisputed letters, he ascribes to Spirit several distinct roles or functions: the Holy Spirit confirms God's love, supports the gospel of God, confirms Christ Jesus, forms and sustains community, and leads Jesus's followers. The Holy Spirit takes on these roles in order to advance the gospel. The purpose of the Spirit is to communicate God's good news to all and sanctify them in Christ. In the community, the Spirit confirms God's love, helps Jesus's followers do his work, and sanctifies them. The Holy Spirit is not a power to be manipulated but rather the presence of God that confirms his good news. Those who follow Jesus and are led by the Spirit may participate in God's love, God's wisdom, and God's power.

QUESTIONS FOR REFLECTION

1. Paul inherited the holy spirit tradition (or the spirit of God) from Jewish scriptures or Jewish tradition. How is his thinking about the holy spirit similar to or different from them?

2. If you translate *pneuma* as breath or wind, does the Holy Breath or Holy Wind make better sense?

3. What is Paul's view of the Spirit? Is it power, the presence of God, or the person?

4. What is the Spirit's relationship with God and Jesus? Is the Holy Spirit different from the Spirit of Jesus? Sometimes, the Spirit is used alone as if it were independent, and at other times, the Spirit is the spirit of God. Do you think Paul has a clear distinction between different uses of the Spirit?

5. How can we discern the work of the Spirit? How can we test the spirit of those who argue that their work comes from the Spirit?

CONCLUSION

Now that the full sweep of Paul's theology has been explored, we can come full circle to issues raised in the introduction. The central concern of Paul's theology is the person and work of Jesus, and if we understand what Paul thinks about Jesus, we unlock the whole of his theology and writing. Paul argues that Jesus is the Son of God whom God sent to do God's work. Jesus demonstrated and thereby revealed God's righteousness. He proclaimed the good news that the world is redeemed through his faithful obedience to God's will. Paul articulates this formula in Rom 3:22: "God's righteousness through Jesus Christ's faithfulness for all who believe" (my translation). God's covenantal faithfulness and God's saving power were confirmed through Jesus's love and grace. Now the power of God is effective for those who have faith—that is, for those who give their loyalty to God through Jesus. God, Paul tells his readers, justifies those who have the faithfulness of Jesus (Rom 3:26). Paul's gospel is "the power of God for salvation to everyone who has faith" (Rom 1:16). In this good news, God's saving grace and covenantal faithfulness are revealed from Jesus's faithfulness and flow to those who share Christ's faithfulness (Rom 1:17). Paul concludes that "the one who is righteous will live by faith" (Rom 1:17; cf. Hab 2:4). If anyone thinks they are righteous, they must live by faith. A righteous person lives faithfully before God and the world. In Paul's theology, faith is not knowledge but rather a person's loyalty, fidelity, and commitment to God demonstrated through following Jesus and his faithfulness. This is how Paul understands Jesus and articulates the significance of Jesus's work.

Paul's role differs from that of Jesus. Paul is not the Messiah or the Son of God. His mission is to proclaim "the good news of God" through "the gospel of Jesus." "The gospel of Jesus" is both the good news that Jesus exemplified and the good news of his grace and sacrifice for the world. Paul's desire is to imitate Christ's faithful life. He expresses this desire in Gal 2:20, writing, "It is no longer I who live, but it is Christ who lives in me. And the life I now live in the flesh I live by *the faithfulness of the Son of God*, who loved me and gave himself for me" (italics indicate my translation).

Despite their distinct identities and roles, both Jesus and Paul have a responsibility to proclaim "the good news of God." In Mark 1:14–15, Jesus begins to proclaim the good news of God after John the Baptist was arrested. He declares that God's time is fulfilled, that God's kingdom has come near, and that people must change their minds and believe in the good news of God. In Rom 1:1, Paul also begins with "the good news of God" and says his calling as an apostle is for this good news, which was promised by God from long ago through his prophets in the holy scriptures (Rom 1:2). God promised the good news to Abraham and all who have faith, as Paul says in Gal 3:8–9: "And the scripture, foreseeing that God would justify the Gentiles by faith, declared the gospel beforehand to Abraham, saying, 'All the Gentiles shall be blessed in you.' For this reason, those who believe are blessed with Abraham who believed." Paul proclaims that God's covenantal faithfulness extends even to the gentiles and argues that all people may become children of God through Christ's act of righteousness (Rom 5:1–21). The good news of God that Christ proclaimed is good news for all who have faith.

In this book, I have tried to deconstruct the many misunderstandings of Paul and his theology. But I did so only to reconstruct his key theological concepts in context. I have tried to examine such concepts within the letters from the context of Paul's ministry. For me, the essence of Paul's preaching hinges on the gospel or good news (*euangelion*), which is the power of God for salvation to everyone who has faith. Paul proclaims the same gospel to each congregation he visits, and it has a threefold structure: God's good news, Christ's good news, and Christian participation in Jesus. In each chapter, I have drawn out the implications of this three-fold gospel. In doing so, I have contrasted Paul's key concepts with those of the Roman Empire and the intellectual, religious, and moral traditions of the Hellenistic world. The good news of God differs starkly from that of Rome. Rome is built by conquest and forced unity. God's good news embraces the marginalized and empowers them. As Paul writes in 1 Cor 1:25–31,

> For God's foolishness is wiser than human wisdom, and God's weakness is stronger than human strength. Consider your own call, brothers and sisters: not many of you were wise by human standards, not many were powerful, not many were of noble birth. But God chose what is foolish in the world to shame the wise; God chose what is weak in the world to shame the strong; God chose what is low and despised in the world, things that are not, to reduce to nothing things that are, so that no one might boast in the presence of God. He is the source of your life in Christ Jesus, who became for us wisdom from God, and righteousness and sanctification and redemption, in order that, as it is written, "Let the one who boasts, boast in the Lord."

The gospel is not mere knowledge about God or Jesus but the power of God that protects the rights of the marginalized and challenges all forms of abusive powers affecting them. Jesus proclaimed this good news of God, and he was crucified for challenging the counterfeit forms of good news that protected the privileged. Paul expanded the notion of good news to include the good news of Christ himself. In Paul's letters, we see that many early Christians did not understand the significance of Jesus's crucifixion, which was the result of his proclamation of God's good news. They did not pay attention to Christ's liberation of the marginalized and instead worked to secure their own status, power, and privilege. Paul implores these Christians to realize God's good news in the world by imitating Jesus and participating in his faithfulness.

The essence of "the gospel of God" is God's righteousness. As Rom 1:17 says, "God's righteousness is revealed from faith to faith" (my translation). "The righteousness of God" in Rom 1:17 and 3:21–22 is God's righteousness, his saving power or covenantal faithfulness that has been extended to the gentiles. The core of Paul's message is about God's righteousness. His theological starting point is not an individual justification but rather God's merciful care and love for all. God's righteousness is revealed from Christ's faithfulness to Christians' faithfulness. "The one who is righteous," Paul says, "will live by faith" (Rom 1:17). God's faithfulness is manifested in his covenant with Abraham and his descendants. It is fulfilled in sending Jesus into the world. We know of God's faithfulness, Paul argues, because Christ's own faithfulness reveals it. The followers of Christ, in turn, reveal Christ's faithfulness to the world by participating in it themselves.

Several further theological concepts flow from Paul's notions of gospel and faith. Freedom is an important topic in Paul's letters. According to Paul, the freedom of the Christian is not the absolute, individual freedom in which a person can think or do anything. Rather, it is the freedom gained by renouncing sin and committing to God. Christ did not walk according to the desire of the flesh but instead sought the will of God according to the Spirit. He defeated sin's temptation and followed God's will. That, for Paul, is freedom. Followers of Jesus may be freed from sin when they follow the example of Jesus. But, being weak, Christians seeking to follow Jesus need the guidance and power of the Spirit to put to death the deeds of the body (Rom 8:13). Freedom, in Paul's theology, has three dimensions. Freedom is *from* something, freedom is *for* something, and freedom is *in* God/Christ. Christians are freed *from* sin, oppression, poverty, ignorance, and hypocrisy. They use that freedom *for* bringing liberation to others. And their freedom is rooted *in* God and *in* Jesus.

New life and new creation are other dominant themes in Paul's thought. Functionally synonyms in Paul's theological

vocabulary, "new life" and "new creation" refer to the ongoing renewal of Christian life and living. It begins when one
comes to Christ and is completed when Christ comes again
in the Parousia. Through Christ's love, one's life takes on a
new meaning oriented by a right relationship with God.
Such a person is called to bless others. Followers of Jesus are
not conquerors. The new life they live and proclaim is not a
weapon. It is liberation.

This book also analyzed the Pauline theme of "the body of
Christ." Paul addresses it in both 1 Cor 12 and Rom 12, and in
both instances, he means more than a community in Christ.
According to traditional interpretation, "the body of Christ" is
understood as a metaphorical organism that emphasizes
communal unity. But I have argued that this interpretation
misses Paul's true meaning and domesticates Paul's message
in order to preserve existing patterns on power and control.
Paul emphasizes not unity but rather union with Christ. In
1 Cor 12:12–27, Christ is ruling over not the members of the
body as a hierarch but rather the whole body in whom all
the members are equal. My critical reimagining of "the body
of Christ" went one step further. I argued that this phrase
must be understood as an attributive genitive: Christlike
body.[15] The Corinthians are the Christic body. They embody
Christ both individually and communally. Through union
with Christ, they are one. This sense of union differs from the
Stoic notion of *homonoia* ("unity" or "concord") in which
the members serve the head. Paul's advice to the Corinthians
is simple: they must follow the way of Christ and have the
same mind as him.

Interpreting Paul will always be contentious. Different people claim different things about him. Some admire him as the
champion of the gospel who proclaimed justification by faith.
Others find in his words the basis for their "forensic" models
of salvation, neglecting the question of believers' participation. The interpretation offered in this book, however, claims

---

15. Since my dissertation and first book in 2008, I have consistently argued that the body
of Christ must be an attributive genitive. See Kim, *Christ's Body in Corinth.*

that "faith in Christ" should be understood as a believer's participation in Christ. Faith, in other words, is not the same as a confession of sins or knowledge about Jesus. It is loyalty and commitment to him. If we understand "faith in Christ" this way, faith does not reject the law or negate Judaism. Rather, it fulfills the law.

Understanding Paul's notion of "the faith/faithfulness of Christ" is the key to understanding justification. Paul's point is not merely that believers have "faith in Christ" but that they have the "faith of Christ" (*pistis christou*). I argued in this book that *pistis christou* must be Christ's faithfulness. This view of faith makes better sense of Paul's writings than the traditional view. Paul is focused in all his undisputed letters on the importance of Christ's love, grace, and sacrifice, which may be summarized in one phrase: *Christ's faith* (Rom 3–8; Gal 1–4; 2 Cor 5). It is almost impossible to talk about Paul's theology without talking about Christ's faithfulness. Christ is everything to Paul because Christ lives in him (Gal 2:20). Paul follows Christ because he was forever changed by Christ's love, faith, and sacrifice. Faith, for Paul, condenses and represents all the works of Jesus. Christ's faith is fidelity or loyalty to God, who promised his good news to the world.

It is important to reclaim Paul's theology of God and Christ and its implications for Christians today. The gospel begins with God, who is our hope and source of life. This is the good news that Jesus proclaimed and confirmed through his love, faith, and sacrifice. This good news is the power of God for salvation for all who have Christ's faith. This faith is participation in Christ and his commitment to God. The goal of the Christian life is to show the love of God to all by following the spirit and example of Jesus. The Holy Spirit is with those who follow Jesus, comforting, aiding, and encouraging them as they go.

BIBLIOGRAPHY

Aristotle. *Nicomachean Ethics*. Internet Classics Archive. Accessed September 28, 2020. https://tinyurl.com/pujm5kw.

———. *On the Generation of Animals*. UNSW Embryology. Accessed September 28, 2020. https://tinyurl.com/y5eces6p.

Arthur, Rose Hofman. *The Wisdom Goddess: Feminist Motifs in Eight Nag Hammadi Documents*. Lanham, MD: University Press of America, 1984.

Badiou, Alain. *Saint Paul: The Foundation of Universalism*. Stanford, CA: Stanford University Press, 2003.

Barclay, John. *Paul and the Gift*. Grand Rapids: Eerdmans, 2017.

Barreto, Eric. "Philemon." In *The New Testament: Fortress Commentary on the Bible*, edited by Margaret Aymer, Cynthia Briggs Kittredge, and David A. Sanchez, 613–623. Minneapolis: Fortress, 2014.

Barrett, C. K. *A Commentary on the First Epistle to the Corinthians*. New York: Harper and Row, 1968.

Bassler, Jouette M. *Navigating Paul: An Introduction to Key Theological Concepts*. Louisville: Westminster John Knox, 2007.

———. "1 Corinthians." In *Women's Bible Commentary*, edited by Carol Newsom and Sharon Ringe, 411–419. Louisville: Westminster John Knox, 1998.

Betz, Hans D. Betz, *Galatians*. Philadelphia: Fortress, 1979.

Bird, Michael. *The Saving Righteousness of God: Studies on Paul, Justification and the New Perspective*. Eugene, OR: Wipf and Stock, 2007.

Black, C. Clifton. "Good News of the New Testament." Bible Odyssey. Accessed January 20, 2020. https://tinyurl.com/yydfa9cc.

Braxton, Brad. "Galatians." In *True to Our Native Land: An African American Commentary of the New Testament*, edited by Brian Blount, Cain Felder, Clarice Martin, and Emerson Powery, 333–347. Minneapolis: Fortress, 2007.

———. *No Longer Slaves: Galatians and African-American Experience.* Collegeville, MN: Liturgical Press, 2002.

———. *The Tyranny of Resolution: 1 Cor 7:17–24.* Atlanta: Society of Biblical Literature, 1999.

Brondos, David. *Paul on the Cross: Reconstructing the Apostle's Story of Redemption.* Minneapolis: Fortress, 2006.

Brooten, Bernadette. "Junia—Outstanding among the Apostles (Romans 6:7)." In *Women Priests: A Catholic Commentary on the Vatican Declaration*, edited by J. Leonard and Arlene Swidler, 141–144. New York: Paulist, 1977.

Cicero. *De Inventione.* University of Waterloo. Accessed September 28, 2020. https://tinyurl.com/y5dszo79.

———. *De Officiis.* Bill Thayer (website). Accessed September 28, 2020. https://tinyurl.com/yx8vr9l8.

Crossan, John Dominic, and Marcus Borg. *The First Paul: Reclaiming the Radical Visionary behind the Church's Conservative Icon.* New York: HarperCollins, 2010.

Culianu, Ioan. "Introduction: The Body Reexamined." In *Religious Reflections on the Human Body*, edited by Jane Marie Law, 1–18. Bloomington: Indiana University Press, 1995.

Digital Dead Sea Scrolls. *The War of the Sons of Light against the Sons of Darkness.* Digital Dead Sea Scrolls. Accessed September 28, 2020. https://tinyurl.com/67p4s6r.

Dittenberger, Wilhelm, comp. *Orientis Graeci Inscriptiones Selectae.* Attalus. Accessed September 28, 2020. https://tinyurl.com/y3occr8z.

Dunn, James. *Jesus, Paul, and the Law: Studies in Mark and Galatians.* Louisville: Westminster John Knox, 1990.

Ehrman, Bart. *The New Testament: A Historical Introduction to the Early Christian Writings.* New York: Oxford University Press, 2016.

Elliott, Neil, and Mark Reasoner, eds. *Documents and Images for the Study of Paul.* Minneapolis: Fortress, 2011.

Epp, Eldon. *Junia: The First Woman Apostle.* Minneapolis: Fortress, 2005.

Fee, Gordon. *God's Empowering Presence: The Holy Spirit in the Letters of Paul.* Peabody, MA: Hendrickson, 1994.

Fitzmyer, Joseph. *First Corinthians: A New Translation with Introduction and Commentary.* New Haven: Yale University Press, 2008.

Fogg, Julia Lambert. "Philippians." In *The New Testament: Fortress Commentary on the Bible*, edited by Margaret Aymer, Cynthia Briggs Kittredge, and David A. Sanchez, 543–556. Minneapolis: Fortress, 2014.

Fredrickson, David. "2 Corinthians." In *The New Testament: Fortress Commentary on the Bible*, edited by Margaret Aymer, Cynthia Briggs Kittredge, and David A. Sanchez, 473–501. Minneapolis: Fortress, 2014.

Furnish, Victor. *2 Corinthians.* Garden City: Doubleday, 1984.

Glancy, Jennifer. *Slavery in Early Christianity.* Minneapolis: Fortress, 2006.

Grieb, Katherine. *The Story of Romans: A Narrative Defense of God's Righteousness.* Louisville: Westminster John Knox, 2002.

Hays, Richard B. *The Faith of Jesus Christ: The Narrative Substructure of Galatians 3:1–4:11.* Grand Rapids: Eerdmans, 2002.

———. "PISTIS and Pauline Christology: What Is at Stake?" In *Pauline Theology*, edited by E. Elizabeth Johnson and David M. Hay, 35–60. Atlanta: Scholars Press, 1997.

Hippocrates. *Places in Man.* Translated by Elizabeth Craik. Oxford: Clarendon, 1998.

Horace. *Odes.* Perseus Digital Library. Accessed September 28, 2020. https://tinyurl.com/y5ppn2k4.

Irenaeus. *Against Heresies.* Early Christian Writings. Accessed September 28, 2020. https://tinyurl.com/oaj4c6b.

Jewett, Robert. *Paul, the Apostle to America: Cultural Trends and Pauline Scholarship.* Louisville: Westminster John Knox, 1994.

———. *Romans: A Commentary.* Minneapolis: Fortress, 2007.

Johnson, Luke Timothy. *Reading Romans: A Literary and Theological Commentary.* Nashville: Abingdon, 2013.

———. "Rom 3:21–26 and the Faith of Jesus." CBQ 44, no. 1 (1982): 77–90.

Josephus. *Jewish War.* Lexundria. Accessed September 28, 2020. https://tinyurl.com/yyc5j9rv.

Kahl, Brigitte. "Galatians." In *The New Testament: Fortress Commentary on the Bible*, edited by Margaret Aymer, Cynthia Briggs

Kittredge, and David A. Sanchez, 503–525. Minneapolis: Fortress, 2014.

Käsemann, Ernst. *New Testament Questions of Today*. Philadelphia: Fortress, 1969.

Keck, Leander E. *Christ's First Theologian: The Shape of Paul's Thought*. Waco, TX: Baylor University Press, 2015.

———. *Romans*. Nashville: Abingdon, 2005.

Kee, Howard. "Aretalogy and Gospel." *JBL* 92 (1973): 402–422.

Keener, Craig S. *1–2 Corinthians*. New York: Cambridge University Press, 2005.

Kim, Yung Suk. "Between Text and Sermon: Hebrews 11:8–16." *Interpretation: A Journal of Bible and Theology* 72, no. 2 (2018): 204–206.

———. *Christ's Body in Corinth: The Politics of a Metaphor*. Minneapolis: Fortress, 2008.

———. "Commentary on 1 Cor 12:1–11." Working Preacher. Accessed September 28, 2020. https://tinyurl.com/yxk7lklf.

———. "Commentary on 1 Cor 13:1–13." Working Preacher. Accessed January 17, 2020. https://tinyurl.com/yyzgk872.

———. *Jesus and Nicodemus*. Anchor FM. March 23, 2020. https://tinyurl.com/y345ap9g.

———. *Jesus's Truth: Life in Parables*. Eugene, OR: Resource, 2018.

———, ed. *1 and 2 Corinthians: Texts at Contexts*. Minneapolis: Fortress, 2013.

———. *Preaching the New Testament Again: Faith, Freedom, and Transformation*. Eugene, OR: Cascade, 2019.

———. "Reclaiming Christ's Body (*soma christou*): Embodiment of God's Gospel in Paul's Letters." *Interpretation* 67, no. 1 (2013): 20–29.

———. *Rereading Galatians from the Perspective of Paul's Gospel: A Literary and Theological Commentary*. Eugene, OR: Cascade, 2019.

———. *Rereading Romans from the Perspective of Paul's Gospel*. Eugene, OR: Resource, 2019.

———. *A Theological Introduction to Paul's Letters: Exploring a Three-fold Theology of Paul*. Eugene, OR: Cascade, 2011.

———. *Truth, Testimony, and Transformation: A New Reading of the "I Am" Sayings of Jesus in the Fourth Gospel*. Eugene, OR: Cascade, 2014.

Kittredge, Cynthia Briggs. "Romans." In *The New Testament: Fortress Commentary on the Bible*, edited by Margaret Aymer, Cynthia

Briggs Kittredge, and David A. Sanchez, 395–426. Minneapolis: Fortress, 2014.

Kraemer, R. S., ed. *Maenads, Martyrs, Matrons, Monastics: A Sourcebook on Women's Religions in the Greco-Roman World.* Minneapolis: Fortress, 1988.

Livy. *History of Rome.* Perseus Digital Library. Accessed September 28, 2020. https://tinyurl.com/y4kd62n4.

Longenecker, Bruce. "PISTIS in Romans 3:25: Neglected Evidence for the Faithfulness of Christ." *New Testament Studies* 39 (1993): 478–480.

Longenecker, Richard. *The Epistle to the Romans.* Grand Rapids: Eerdmans, 2016.

Mafico, Temba L. J. "Just, Justice." In *Anchor Bible Dictionary*, edited by David Noel Freedman, 1127–1129. Vol. 3. New York: Doubleday, 1992.

Manilius. *Astronomica.* Translated by G. P. Goold. Cambridge, MA: Harvard University Press, 1977.

Martin, Dale. *The Corinthian Body.* New Haven: Yale University Press, 1995.

———. *Slavery as Salvation: The Metaphor of Slavery in Pauline Christianity.* New Haven: Yale University Press, 1990.

Martyn, J. Louis. "A Law-Observant Messiah to the Gentiles." *Scottish Journal of Theology* 38 (1985): 307–324.

McKnight, Scott, and Joseph Modica, eds. *Preaching Romans: Four Perspectives.* Grand Rapids: Eerdmans, 2019.

Meggitt, Justin. *Paul, Poverty, and Survival.* Edinburgh: T&T Clark, 1998.

Miguéz, Néstor Oscar. "Galatians." In the *Global Bible Commentary*, edited by Daniel Patte, 463–472. Nashville: Abingdon, 2004.

Mitchell, Margaret. *Paul and the Rhetoric of Reconciliation: An Exegetical Investigation of the Language and Composition of 1 Corinthians.* Louisville: Westminster John Knox, 1987.

Nasrallah, Laura. "1 Corinthians." In *The New Testament: Fortress Commentary on the Bible*, edited by Margaret Aymer, Cynthia Briggs Kittredge, and David A. Sanchez, 427–471. Minneapolis: Fortress, 2014.

Neyrey, Jerome. *Paul in Other Words: A Cultural Reading of His Letter.* Louisville: Westminster John Knox, 1990.

Nongbri, Brent. "2 Corinthians and Possible Material Evidence for Composite Letters in Antiquity." In *Collecting Early Christian Letters: From the Apostle Paul to Late Antiquity*, edited by B. Neil and P. Allen, 54–67. Cambridge: Cambridge University Press, 2015.

O'Connor-Murphy, Jerome. "1 Corinthians 11:2–16 Once Again." CBQ 50 (1988): 265–274.

Odell-Scott, David. "Let the Women Speak in Church: An Egalitarian Interpretation of 1 Cor 14:33b–36." *Biblical Theology Bulletin* 13 (1983): 90–93.

———. *Paul's Critique of Theocracy: A/Theocracy in Corinthians and Galatians*. New York: T&T Clark, 2003.

Osiek, Carolyn. "Galatians." In *The Women's Bible Commentary*, edited by Carol A. Newsom and Sharon Ringe, 333–337. Louisville: Westminster John Knox, 1992.

Patte, Daniel. "Romans." In the *Global Bible Commentary*, edited by Daniel Patte, 429–443. Nashville: Abingdon, 2004.

Philo. *On Abraham*. Early Christian Writings. Accessed September 28, 2020. https://tinyurl.com/y5jnkjwz.

———. *On the Giants*. Early Christian Writings. Accessed September 28, 2020. https://tinyurl.com/yy6y9txq.

———. *On the Life of Moses*. Early Jewish Writings. Accessed September 28, 2020. https://tinyurl.com/y6rd8lr2.

———. *Questions and Answers on Genesis*. Early Jewish Writings. Accessed September 28, 2020. https://tinyurl.com/y5mrksfj.

———. *The Special Laws*. Early Jewish Writings. Accessed September 28, 2020. https://tinyurl.com/yyd2oew.

Pillar, Edward. "1 Thessalonians." In *The New Testament: Fortress Commentary on the Bible*, edited by Margaret Aymer, Cynthia Briggs Kittredge, and David A. Sanchez, 573–582. Minneapolis: Fortress, 2014.

Plato. *Laws*. Perseus Digital Library. Accessed September 28, 2020. https://tinyurl.com/y2opnou8.

———. *Republic*. Perseus Digital Library. Accessed September 28, 2020. https://tinyurl.com/h5alxu4.

———. *Timaeus*. Perseus Digital Library. Accessed September 28, 2020. https://tinyurl.com/yxbfmrhc.

Pliny. *Letters*. Attalus. Accessed September 28, 2020. https://tinyurl.com/y3fje6tz.

Powell, Mark Allan. *Fortress Introduction to the Gospels.* 2nd ed. Minneapolis: Fortress, 2019.

Price, James L. "God's Righteousness Shall Prevail." *Interpretation* 28, no. 3 (1974): 259–280.

Reasoner, Mark. *Romans in Full Circle: A History of Interpretation.* Louisville: Westminster John Knox, 2005.

Roetzel, Calvin. *The Letters of Paul: Conversations in Context.* Louisville: Westminster John Knox, 1998.

Sanders, Boykin. "1 Corinthians." In *True to Our Native Land: An African American Commentary of the New Testament,* edited by Brian Blount, Cain Felder, Clarice Martin, and Emerson Powery, 276–306. Minneapolis: Fortress, 2007.

Sanders, E. P. *Comparing Judaism and Christianity: Common Judaism, Paul, and the Inner and the Outer in Ancient Religion.* Minneapolis: Fortress, 2016.

———. *Paul and Palestinian Judaism: A Comparison of Patterns of Religion.* Philadelphia: Fortress, 1977.

———. *Paul: The Apostle's Life, Letters, and Thought.* Minneapolis: Fortress, 2015.

Scullion, John. "Righteousness (OT)." In *Anchor Bible Dictionary,* edited by David Noel Freedman, 724–736. Vol. 5. New York: Doubleday, 1992.

Sechrest, Love. "Identity and Embodiment of Privilege in Corinth." In *1-2 Corinthians,* edited by Yung Suk Kim, 9–30. Minneapolis: Fortress, 2013.

Seneca. *De beneficiis.* Stoics. Accessed September 28, 2020. https://tinyurl.com/yxr2d5st.

———. *Epistles.* Stoic Therapy. Accessed September 28, 2020. https://tinyurl.com/y2be9cf9.

Smith, Daniel. *Into the World of the New Testament: Greco-Roman and Jewish Texts and Contexts.* New York: T&T Clark, 2015.

———. "Why Paul's Fabulous Body Is Missing Its Belly: The Rhetorical Subversion of Menenius Agrippa's Fable in 1 Corinthians 12.12–30." *Journal for the Study of the New Testament* 41, no. 2 (2018): 143–160.

Smith, Mitzi J. "Slavery in the Early Church." In *True to Our Native Land: An African American Commentary of the New Testament,* edited by Brian Blount, Cain Felder, Clarice Martin, and Emerson Powery, 11–22. Minneapolis: Fortress, 2007.

Smith, Mitzi, and Yung Suk Kim. *Toward Decentering the New Testament: A Reintroduction.* Eugene, OR: Cascade, 2018.

Smith, Morton. "Prolegomena to a Discussion of Aretalogies, Divine Men, the Gospels, and Jesus." *JBL* 90 (1971): 174–199.

Stendahl, Krister. "The Apostle Paul and the Introspective Conscience of the West." *Harvard Theological Review* 56, no. 3 (1963): 199–215.

Stowers, Stanley. *A Rereading of Romans: Justice, Jews and Gentiles.* New Haven: Yale University Press, 1994.

Talbert, Charles H. *Romans.* Macon, GA: Smyth & Helwys, 2002.

Taylor, N. H. "The Composition and Chronology of Second Corinthians." *Journal for the Study of the New Testament* 14, no. 44 (1991): 67–87.

Thieselton, Anthony. *The First Epistle to the Corinthians.* Grand Rapids: Eerdmans, 2000.

Trombley, Frank. "Prolegomena to the Systemic Analysis of Late Hellenistic Religion: The Case of the Aretalogy of Isis at Kyme." In *Religious Writings and Religious Systems*, edited by J. Neusner, E. S. Frerichs, and A. J. Levine, 95–113. Atlanta: Scholars Press, 1989.

Trompf, Garry. "On Attitudes toward Women in Paul and Paulinist Literature: 1 Corinthians 11:3–16 and Its Context." *CBQ* 42 (1980): 196–215.

Twelftree, Graham. *The Gospel According to Paul: A Reappraisal.* Eugene, OR: Cascade, 2019.

Walker, Wm. "1 Corinthians and Paul's Views regarding Women." *JBL* 94 (1974): 94–110.

Welborn, Laurence L. *Paul, the Fool of Christ: A Study of 1 Corinthians 1–4 in the Comic-Philosophic Tradition.* New York: T&T Clark, 2005.

Williams, Demetrius K. "'No Longer as a Slave': Reading the Interpretation History of Paul's Epistle to Philemon." In *Onesimus Our Brother: Reading Religion, Race, and Culture in Philemon*, edited by Matthew Johnson, James Noel, and Demetrius Williams, 11–45. Minneapolis: Fortress, 2012.

Wills, Garry. *What Paul Meant.* New York: Penguin, 2006.

Wire, Antoinette. *The Corinthian Women Prophets: A Reconstruction through Paul's Rhetoric.* Minneapolis: Fortress, 1990.

Works, Carla. *The Least of These: Paul and the Marginalized.* Grand Rapids: Eerdmans, 2020.

Yamaguchi, Satoko. "'I Am' Sayings and Women in Context." In *A Feminist Companion to John*, edited by Amy-Jill Levine, 35–40. Sheffield: Sheffield Academic Press, 2003.

Yeo, K. K., ed. *Navigating Romans through Cultures: Challenging Readings by Charting a New Course*. New York: T&T Clark, 2004.

Zetterholm, Magnus. *Approaches to Paul: A Student's Guide to Recent Scholarship*. Minneapolis: Fortress, 2009.

SUBJECT INDEX

SCRIPTURE INDEX

OLD TESTAMENT

APOCRYPHA

NEW TESTAMENT